TEACHING Youth WITH CONFIDENCE

by
Harley Atkinson, Ph.D.

Evangelical Training Association

110 Bridge Street • Box 327

Wheaton, IL 60189-0327

Cover Design: Kurtz Design Studio, Tulsa, OK

2001 Edition, First Printing

ISBN: 1-929852-00-2

Contents

The Challenge of Teaching Youth

1

Teaching is a universal phenomenon. In every historical era and in every culture, teaching has been or is currently taking place. Parents teach children, school teachers instruct young learners, employers teach workers, college professors instruct students, and youth workers teach adolescents. However, while teaching is a common occurrence, it can also be an awesome and urgent task—especially in the case of teaching teenagers.

Although teaching teenagers can be an immensely rewarding ministry, anyone who has taught young people also knows it can be extremely disappointing and, at times, beset with considerable frustrations—lack of motivation to learn, disinterest in spiritual matters, stubborn resistance, and even outright rebelliousness and hostility on the part of youth. In addition, teaching contemporary youth can be especially challenging and demanding. Teenagers today are beseiged with numerous critical issues which make it apparent that surviving this phase of life is growing increasingly difficult. Thus, it is the critical responsibility of those who work with teenagers to bring the Word of God to them in a manner that permeates their entire beings and radically transforms their lives.

The Challenge of Understanding Contemporary Life

The most casual glance at today's newspaper or a cursory viewing of the evening times will reveal the enormous cultural influences impacting youth today. Some of the significant trends that uniquely shape this generation of adolescents are here briefly identified.

Mobility

Americans are among the most mobile people in the world. This mobility affords teenagers special opportunities, but it also creates difficulties for some youth. The advantages of frequent moving are that it provides them with broader life experiences and varied opportunities for growth and learning. The drawbacks of mobility include dismay over losing friends, the fear of developing new friendships, and feelings of instability due to the frequent changing of schools and youth groups. All of this is taking place at a stage in life when adolescents are going through radical internal personal changes and are in need of models of stability.

Knowledge and Technology Explosion

Unless interrupted by a major catastrophe, the volume of knowledge and information available to man will continue to increase at a colossal rate. Scientific and technological knowledge bases will continue to multiply with each passing year. While technology in an of itself is not wrong, the technological influence of contemporary America can deprive youth of a sense of belonging and community and threaten them with depersonalization. For example, where television, electronic games, and computers rule the home, families tend to have fewer family discussions and spend less recreation time together. Those who teach youth have the huge responsibility of demonstrating the immensely personal love of Jesus Christ in a knowledge-saturated and technological-bound culture where youth are longing for meaningful relationships and a sense of belonging.

Mass media

Teenagers are increasingly influenced by television and other mass media. Through mass media, adolescents are exposed to varieties of ideologies, lifestyles, and value systems that are antithetical to biblical principles. The effect of media (whether intentional or not) is to form individuals who do not, or cannot, think for themselves but are programmed to react unconsciously in a determined way. In addition to television and its countless channel offerings, movies, various forms of advertising, music, and the Internet all vie for the attention of the youth population.

Ethnic Diversity

At the turn of the twentieth century, European immigration to the United States peaked as people fled starvation, poverty, and war. America offered hope and opportunity and was seen as a great "melting pot" where people from many lands melted, or blended, into a new American society. Now America is often described as a multicultural society that is more like a "salad bowl" than a melting pot. Today, immigrants are more likely to be Asians or Hispanics than Europeans. Many youth groups will be increasingly diverse ethnically, a pattern that will pose special challenges to youth workers, causing them to wrestle with the biblical axiom that in Christ there is neither Jew nor Greek, while at the same time celebrating racial diversity and encouraging ethnic identity.

Postmodernism

Young people today are growing up in what philosophers call a postmodern world. According to the postmodern mindset, there is no claim to absolute truth or meaning in life; instead, truth is defined by each individual or by the community he or she belongs to. Many young people (both churched and unchurched) are confused about what truth is or simply do not accept an absolute truth, or a truth that is unchanging, universal, eternal, and objective. Consequently, youth are reacting to a worldview characterized by chaos and pessimism. These youth are the products of broken homes and the victims of violence, mired in a sea of uncertainty. The critical challenges for youth workers are to reclaim this lost generation for Jesus Christ and to help teenagers once again learn how to determine right from wrong.

Rapid Social Change

In 1970, sociologist Alvin Toffler predicted that in the subsequent years, people would experience social and technological change so intense and rapid that they would suffer a malady he called "future shock." He characterized this psychological abnormality as being similar to, but more profound than, the culture shock often experienced when visiting foreign countries.[1] This rapidly changing social system has arrived and is so powerful that it creates a milieu significantly different from the milieu of each preceding generation. One of the consequences of this rapid change is that each generation of adults finds it increasingly difficult to understand the current generation of youth, and likewise, youth find it increasingly difficult to understand adults, viewing their parents or the previous generation as old-fashioned or totally disconnected from the current times.

Family Breakdown

In the United States, the family social unit has undergone significant structural and functional change in the last three decades. The rise in the divorce rate, the growing number of out-of-wedlock births, and the declining number of marriages have all contributed to the altered composition of the family. The challenge for churches and youth workers now and in the near future will be to strengthen the family and to help young people cope with the negative effects of family breakdown.

The Challenge of Understanding Adolescence

The adolescent years are dynamic, unpredictable, and demanding, and for many youth, it is a particularly difficult and tumultuous stage of life. Many physical, mental, and social changes occur in a relatively short period of time, and numerous significant decisions are made. Young people not only need help in understanding themselves, but they require special guidance in making life-changing decisions. Many youth make a first time decision to accept Christ as Savior, and those who received Him earlier in life come to recognize Him as Lord of their lives and so propose to live for Him more fully.

Physical and Mental Change

The physical changes that a young adolescent experiences are second only to those which occur in the initial years of life. Rapid growth spurts characterize the preadolescent and early adolescent years of both boys and girls. During puberty, young teens experience the emergence of secondary sex characteristics such as facial and body hair for boys, breast development and body hair for girls, and maturation of sexual organs for both genders. Mental or cognitive skills are changing as well. Young teens begin to develop the capacity to think more abstractly and are less bound to the here and now in thought. Abstract thinking skills allow them to imagine the ideal and to compare reality with fantasized perfection.

Growth in Independence

Youth are in a season of growth in independence and in the establishing of a personal identity. As they assert themselves and spread their wings, the teacher has an opportunity to assist them in learning the values of both independence and interdependence. Young people can learn about the strengths, gifts, and capabilities they have which contribute to their personal being and their identity. At the same time, they must learn how to use these strengths and abilities to benefit others and strengthen their communities.

Career Choices

Career choices are often made, or at least considered, in the teen years. Teachers can assist teenagers as they consider their abilities and interests in regard to their future in the work world and in relation to what they can do for Christ. This is an appropriate time to teach a theological understanding of the will of God and to instruct young people on how to make significant life decisions.

Marriage

With the decline and breakdown of the traditional family, helping teenagers develop a sound biblical perspective of dating, marriage relationships, and the home is an exciting challenge to any teacher of youth. As teachers bring the Scripture to bear on such issues, they can assist in the development of much needed biblically-based values. This, in turn, will help youth establish relationships that are truly meaningful and will ultimately aid them in building homes based on God's principles.

Social Relationships

Adolescence is also a season of social growth and change. While the family is always the most important social unit for individuals, from childhood onward, peers and friends play an increasingly significant role in life experience. Abilities to be more transparent and to communicate on deeper levels enhance a youth's ability to nurture meaningful relationships with both peers and adults. What an occasion for the opportunistic youth worker to teach friendship and communication skills, the dangers of negative peer pressure, and the values of positive peer influence!

Critical Issues

While adolescence is a period of tremendous growth and development, it is also a time when young people are confronted with a myriad of life-endangering concerns and critical issues. For instance, young people are experimenting with illicit drugs and alcohol at increasingly younger ages. Many of them are also choosing to engage in premarital sex, leading to a rise in unwanted pregnancies, abortions, single parenthood, and sexually transmitted diseases. Even more disheartening, the rate of suicide for adolescents has quadrupled since 1950, and it has become the third leading cause of death for this age group. Teenagers also continue to face threats in the form of school violence and various forms of physical and sexual abuse. Youth teachers have an opportunity like never before to offer support and care to teens who struggle with these kinds of critical issues.

The Challenge of Teaching

Teaching is a formidable task, and quality teaching requires a working understanding of the complexities of the teaching-learning process. Dynamic and meaningful teaching must take into consideration a number of components: the Holy Spirit, the class objectives, the teacher, the learner, the curriculum, the environment, and the methods. Furthermore, it is important to understand what teaching is and what it is not. Dynamic teaching is not simply covering the curriculum or passing on biblical facts and doctrine. To be sure, Bible content and doctrine are essential, but teaching is much more than passing on information. Effective teachers of youth hope to see young lives changed, to see youth experience intimacy with Christ, and to help youth discover and use their gifts for the Kingdom.

Conclusion

Young people represent a treasure to the Church. These gems may be rough, uncut, and unpolished, but they are jewels of inestimable value. God places a high value on youth in His Word. He uses young people to share His truth and to illustrate His principles, as we see from Joseph in Genesis 37, David and Jonathan in 1 Samuel 20, and Daniel and His three friends in Daniel 1-3. In the New Testament, sections of the Epistles were written directly to youth (1 Tim. 5:1, Titus 2:4-6, 1 Pet. 5:5, and 1 John 2:13-14). Finally, a great challenge for youth to be Christlike is found in 1 Timothy 4:12: "Let no one look down on your youthfulness, but rather in speech, conduct, love, faith and purity, show yourself an example of those who believe" (NASB).

Rising to the challenge of teaching youth begins with a vision for youth education and a high priority for youth on the part of each teacher and youth ministry leader. It begins with a careful look at what an effective teacher of youth is. It means a willingness to grow in an understanding of adolescents and the complex world in which they live. It also means taking the time to learn about the various elements of the teaching-learning process and mastering the techniques of dynamic teaching.

For Further Discussion

1. Which aspect of teaching youth do you find most challenging?
2. Which trend in contemporary life has affected your own ministry to youth the most?
3. What are some evidences that your church or ministry places a high value on youth? Could it be doing more to this effect?

Notes

1. Alvin Toffler, *Future Shock* (New York: Bantam Books, 1970), 10-11.

Teaching With Focus

2

Any successful organization or ministry has a clear indication of why it exists and what it wants to accomplish. Dann Spader of Sonlife Ministries says, "The ability to succeed and to measure success is directly tied to a clear and focused understanding of our mission— **why do we exist?** A slight shift in purpose can greatly alter what we do and why we do it."[1] If clear expectations of an educational ministry can be defined, the appropriate strategies and learning experiences can be determined. Furthermore, a clearly defined purpose and a set of well-defined aims give us a standard whereby we can measure our effectiveness.

The Purpose of Youth Education

In order to get a sense of direction in youth educational ministries, youth workers must ask the question, "What are we trying to do with our teenagers?" If this question was posed to a number of youth workers or teachers, they would surely give a variety of answers, and it is rather certain most of these would be in some manner on target. However, it seems clear the one overall or sole purpose of youth education is to fulfill the biblical mandate of Christ to change lives by making disciples (Matt. 28:18-20).

What is a disciple? Gary Kuhne proposes this definition: "A disciple is a Christian who is growing in conformity to Christ, is achieving fruit in evangelism, and is working in follow-up to conserve his fruits."[2] Note that a disciple is not a super Christian, a unique individual, or an expert. The biblical notion of a disciple (*mathetes*) is that of a learner. Disciples are simply believers who are growing in conformity to Jesus Christ. An overarching purpose of teaching youth, then, is discipleship training, or the "work of developing spiritual maturity and spiritual reproductiveness" in the lives of teenage Christians.[3]

Aims and Objectives of Teaching Youth

With a distinct purpose of making disciples in mind, youth teachers are then ready to develop an additional number of aims or objectives that enable them to achieve that purpose. The following list includes a number of objectives for which every teacher of youth should strive.

That Youth Are Brought Into a Saving Relationship With Christ

One of the first concerns of the Christian teacher of youth is to bring young people into a saving relationship with Jesus Christ. After all, how can spiritual nurture or discipleship take place if teens have not first received spiritual life through regeneration? Dann Spader identifies seven principles helpful in developing a heart for lost teenagers.[4]

1. *Jesus Christ is the only way whereby an individual can be restored in his or her relationship with God (John 14:6; 1 Tim. 2:5).*
2. *Evangelism is the heartbeat of God. First Timothy 2:4 says God "wants all men to be saved and to come to a knowledge of the truth."*
3. *Evangelism is a privilege. The Creator of the universe has chosen us as His ambassadors to proclaim the Good News of Christ and to touch others' lives (Matt. 4:19).*
4. *Evangelism is most effective when it is done out of a motivation of love (Phil. 1:15-18).*
5. *Effective evangelism is the outcome of a healthy church body (Acts 2:42-47).*
6. *Evangelism is a process, rather than an event. Young people are at different stages in the process of coming to a saving relationship with Jesus Christ.*
7. *Evangelism is most effective when done through friendships.*

That Youth Acquire a Personalized, Firsthand Faith

Definitions abound, but at the heart of the understanding of what faith is, lies the notion of believing in or adhering to a specific set of doctrines and values. Though faith is believing, it is also a way of living; it is allowing those beliefs to shape one's life. Faith of early adolescence tends to be constituted of values and beliefs acquired from others—parents, pastors, youth workers, Sunday School teachers, and other important figures. One of the critical tasks of the youth teacher is to enable Christian teenagers to work towards personalizing their faith, to acquire what youth ministry expert Duffy Robbins calls a *firsthand faith.*[5]

That Youth Gain Knowledge and Understanding of Biblical Truth (2 Tim. 3:16; 1 Pet. 2:2)

It is imperative young people know and understand the foundational truths of Scripture. How will teenagers know right from wrong if they do not understand biblical precepts? How can their lives be transformed if they do not learn to interact with the Word? Peter advises his readers, "Crave pure spiritual milk, so that by it you may grow up in your salvation" (1 Pet. 2:2), and Paul reminds his audience that "all Scripture is God-breathed and is useful for teaching, rebuking, correcting and training in righteousness" (2 Tim. 3:16).

Unfortunately, it appears that most contemporary churched youth are ambivalent and confused about truth. According to a study done by Josh McDowell and Bob Hostetler, more than half of youth acknowledge the existence of truth in certain circumstances but later deny that view when the question is worded differently. For instance, 72 percent say that the Bible provides a clear and indisputable description of moral truth, yet only 44 percent affirmed that humans are capable of grasping the meaning of truth.[6] Christian young people are growing up in a climate where the possibility of knowing absolute truth is denied. Allan Bloom, in his opening statement of *The Closing of the American Mind,* asserts, "There is one thing a professor can be absolutely certain of: almost every student entering the university believes, or says he believes, that truth is relative."[7]

Although teaching the Word is a crucial component of youth ministry, knowledge of the Bible is not an end in itself. The New Testament author James writes, "Do not merely listen to the word, and so deceive yourselves. Do what it says" (1:22). Rather, biblical content is given as a means to bring individuals into a right relationship with God and to provide answers to the questions and issues of daily living. Lois LeBar reminds us that it is "possible to starve people with biblical facts, to make doctrine a substitute for spiritual reality, to fail our people by denying them the intimate personal experience with the Lord Himself who alone will satisfy the deepest longings of the human heart."[8]

That Youth Be Able to Apply Biblical Truths to Life Issues

Since teaching for biblical knowledge alone is insufficient, the teacher must develop further aims. One such aim is enabling young people to bring biblical truth to bear on life issues. They must see how the timeless truths of Scripture relate to their current needs and experiences. Each youth should learn to ask questions like these: What do I do when someone wants to copy my answers at school? What do I do when I am watching a movie and a sexually explicit scene comes on? What kind of music is appropriate or inappropriate? Should I date a non-Christian? What does the Bible say about suicide? What does it say on issues such as homosexuality, war, abortion, or poverty?

It is the responsibility of the teacher to help his or her students respond to these urgent life-related issues in a biblical way. James Plueddemann offers the "Rail-Fence Model" to depict the relationship between the Word and the student. The fence is constructed of two rails held together by fence posts (see Figure 2). The upper rail represents Truth, while the lower rail stands for life. Anything that connects the upper rail of Truth with the lower rail of life is a fence post: an insight a learner discovers concerning the relationship between a biblical principle and a life need, particular methods, or critical reflection.[9]

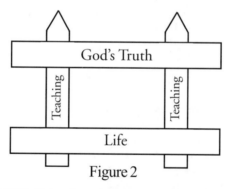

Figure 2

That Youth Will Grow Into Maturity in Jesus Christ (Eph. 4:13)

Another aim of youth education is to see spiritual growth take place in the individual lives of teenagers. The Apostle Paul desires that all believers "reach unity in the faith and in the knowledge of the Son of God and become mature" (Eph. 4:13). In subsequent phrases and verses, Paul indicates what spiritual maturity is.

"The whole measure of the fullness of Christ" (4:13). Christ is the measure at which young people are to aim. While we rightly encourage youth workers, teachers, and parents to serve as models of Christlike living, ultimately the rule or measure for righteousness is Jesus Christ Himself. An accurate understanding of who Christ is, is absolutely essential to a teenager's growth and development. Furthermore, a proper motivation to serve and minister is derived from a correct understanding of Jesus Christ.

"We will no longer be infants" (4:14). Here Paul is using the term "infant" to refer to spiritual immaturity—an immaturity that is understandable when an individual is very young or new in the faith. However, Paul insists that one must grow out of this infancy, not content to remain in this state of immaturity. Spiritual maturity comes not with the childish naiveté that is "tossed back and forth by the waves, and blown here and there by every wind of teaching" (Eph. 4:14), but, as Duffy Robbins explains, it is a "faith that is tough enough to stay afloat in the midst of the storms and waves of real life with real questions."[10]

Able to withstand "the cunning and craftiness of men in their deceitful scheming" (Eph. 4:14b). Paul identifies an additional concern of spiritual growth when he writes that spiritual immaturity is characterized by the inability to withstand the "cunning and craftiness of men in their deceitful scheming." Duffy Robbins rightly contexualizes this verse by reminding us that "teenagers are easily victimized by that which looks true and sounds true, but is not true. An important facet of spiritual growth is gaining the ability to discern between that which is true and that which is false."[11]

"From him the whole body, joined and held together by every supporting ligament, grows and builds itself up in love, as each part does its work" (Eph. 4:16). Note that Paul is very careful to place personal growth in the context of relationships. "Relating," declares Julie Gorman, "is at the heart of knowing God. Relating is also at the heart of becoming the people of God. Our faith journey is one we make together. Community is the context for our growth."[12] One of the best ways to enable teenagers to grow spiritually is to involve them with their peers who are growing in spiritual maturity.[13]

That Youth Be Equipped For Ministry and Service (Eph. 4:12)

One of the targeted goals for all believers is that they be equipped or prepared to do the work of ministry and service. Youth programs err seriously when they provide entertainment, activities, and ministries for their young people but fail to prepare them for service or to provide opportunities for them to minister. There are those who will disagree, but junior and senior high school teenagers can be ministers and they should be trained as such. What are some ministries teenagers can be equipped for? The list is not exhaustive, but consider the following possibilities: leading Bible studies or small groups, planning and organizing activities, witnessing, hospital visitation, peer counseling, visiting shut-ins, leading worship, leading meetings, teaching, welcoming visitors, preaching, facilitating worship, leading prayer groups, and discipling one-on-one.

Conclusion

Anyone who has spent any time in the construction business learns quickly that in order to effectively construct a house or set of apartments, one first has to have a set of blueprints. In other words, one must begin building with a clear and accurate picture of what the completed work should look like. So it is with nurturing youth. The successful teacher must have a clear picture or blueprint of what the finished product will look like.

The end products of successful teaching ministries are discipled youth. What do discipled youth look like? They should exhibit the following characteristics: a personal relationship with Jesus Christ, a personalized faith, a knowledge and understanding of the Word of God, an ability to apply biblical truths to life issues, a maturity in Jesus Christ, and a life that is equipped for ministry and service.

For Further Discussion

1. Have you ever been part of a ministry that lacked a clear focus? What were the results?
2. How well is your ministry doing in making youth disciples? In what objectives are you the strongest/weakest?
3. Develop a blueprint of a discipled youth in your class. How far is the ideal from reality? What would it take to make it a reality?

Notes

1. Dann Spader, *The Sonlife Strategy* (Elburn, Ill.: Sonlife Ministries, 1993),12.
2. Gary W. Kuhne, *The Dynamics of Personal Follow-up* (Grand Rapids: Zondervan, 1976), 21.
3. Ibid., 22.
4. Spader, 12.
5. Duffy Robbins, *The Ministry of Nurture,* 59.
6. Josh McDowell and Bob Hostetler, *Right From Wrong,* 15.
7. Allan Bloom, *The Closing of the American Mind* (New York: Simon & Schuster, 1987), 25.
8. Lois E. LeBar and James E. Plueddemann, *Education That is Christian,* 24.
9. Ibid., 105-6. Plueddemann credits Ted Ward and Sam Rowen for first developing the rail fence analogy as a model for Theological Education by Extension.
10. Robbins, 26.
11. Ibid.
12. Julie A. Gorman, *Community That is Christian,* 23.
13. Robbins, 26.

The Dynamic Teacher of Youth

$\mathcal{3}$

The well-known psychologist Carl Rogers allegedly described teaching as a relatively unimportant and vastly over-valued activity. Is teaching unimportant to learning? Does the teacher fill an insignificant or even a dispensable role? Some Christians would agree, in a sense, with Rogers. They argue that human teachers are unnecessary and that all one needs in order to learn the Word of God is the teaching power of the Holy Spirit. However, both views are insufficient. Christian teachers are absolutely necessary to the lifeblood of the Church and the perpetuation of the Christian faith. The great reformer Martin Luther held a high view of the profession of teaching and asserted that, next to the work of preaching, teaching was dearest to the heart of God. Christ, at the end of His earthly ministry, commanded His disciples to, in turn, "make disciples of all nations . . . teaching them to obey everything I have commanded you" (Matt. 28:19-20). The Apostle Paul includes teachers as those given by Christ to help prepare God's people for works of service and the building up of the body (Eph. 4:11-12). He also identifies teaching as one of the spiritual gifts (Rom. 12:7).

Characteristics of the Teacher

The youth teacher has the awesome responsibility and privilege of investing his or her life in the lives of teenagers. However, not all possess the characteristics or skills necessary to be effective as teachers of youth. What are some characteristics that are found in dynamic teachers?

17

A Close Relationship With Jesus Christ

What teenagers need from teachers today, more than anything else, are authentic men and women who model consistent, godly, Spirit-filled lives. The youth teacher should be able to say as Paul did: "Follow my example, as I follow the example of Christ" (1 Cor. 11:1). Young people today are tired of adults who preach or teach one message and practice a lifestyle that is inconstant with that message. What teenagers want to see is authenticity. They are seeking answers to life's critical issues and need to see values in operation. It is crucial that they see, as well as hear, how the Word of God can and does affect every area of life.

A Heart for Youth

Jesus models for us a heart of compassion and endless love for people. He instructed His disciples that "the Son of Man did not come to be served, but to serve, and to give his life as a ransom for many" (Matt. 20:28). In the same way, teachers must exhibit a sincere compassion and love for young people. If there is one thing teenagers today are desperately searching for, it is to be loved. Yet teens are often difficult to love—some more than others. Mark Twain captured the sentiments of most adults (including many youth workers) when he said that once a child reaches twelve, we should put him in a barrel with a small hole in the side to feed him, and when he reaches sixteen, we should plug up the hole. Indeed, many adolescents are caustic, apathetic, or just downright rude. But Jesus loved the unlovely, and He expects no less from those who work with youth.

Biblical and Theological Knowledge

Teenagers will ask tough questions. They will challenge the authority of Scripture, the existence of God, or the nature of the Trinity. Furthermore, they will seek answers to critical issues such as abortion, suicide, or premarital sex. If teachers are not able to provide adequate answers, students will conclude there are none. This does not mean that we should quickly give them answers to all their questions (we should also allow them to dig for themselves). It does, however, mean we should be familiar enough with the Word of God, theological teachings, and basic issues of apologetics so we can help teens deal with their questions in an intellectually responsible way.

Knowledge of the Learner

One of the reasons Jesus' teaching was so dynamic was that He knew and understood His pupils. When the Pharisees claimed Jesus performed miracles by the power of Beelzebub, the Bible says He knew their thoughts (Matt. 12:24-25). Jesus knew Nathanael while he was still afar off (John 1:47-48), and He was able to tell the Samaritan woman at the well all about her personal life upon their first encounter (John 4:29). While teachers may not have the divine ability to discern the thoughts of others, they can know their learners in other ways. First, the teacher can know them from a developmental perspective, which involves understanding adolescence as a stage of life. Second, the teacher can know teenagers by understanding youth culture—knowing about the world in which they live. Third, the teacher can know his or her learners personally—their family life, their personal struggles, the music they listen to, their hobbies, their aspirations, and their likes, dislikes, and interests.

Teaching Ability and Expertise

Finally, the teacher must know how to teach. C. V. Eavey says, "There never was a teacher who was more fully led by the Holy Spirit than was our Lord Jesus Christ, and yet none ever observed the laws of teaching more consistently."[1] Some teaching skills that will be addressed later in this book are an ability to create a warm and accepting climate for learning, creativity, and the abilities to communicate clearly, to use a variety of methods, and to teach for higher levels of thinking.

Roles of the Teacher

In addition to the characteristics and skills of the effective teacher, there are several significant roles which the teacher must perform successfully.

Model

Modeling is one of the primary roles of adult youth workers, and the most effective teachers are ones who exemplify the subject matter they present in class. Donald Posterski encourages those who aspire to teach youth to ponder the question, "Does my behavior deserve to be duplicated?" He goes on to say that adults who serve the best interests of young people are those who model what is important and lead the way with their living.[2] The youth teacher must surely know the message, but more importantly, he or she must *be* the message. For as Herman Horne remarks, "It is a pedagogical truism that we teach more by what we are than what we say."[3]

Guide

In her insightful book *Education That is Christian,* Lois LeBar likens teaching to conducting a guided tour.[4] The competent guide is one who has previously taken the trip (perhaps many times) and is familiar with the points of interest and significant places to visit. The guide plans the itinerary, makes arrangements, and then leads the tourists into a firsthand experience of these places. Imagine a tour guide saying to the tourists, "Since I've been there before, I'll just tell you about the experience." This would be absurd, yet this is what many teachers of youth do. They have enjoyed the rich experience of learning truth firsthand from God's Word, and rather than guiding young people into that same experience, they shortcut the teaching/learning process by merely telling. As youth seek to know truth and apply it to their lives, they need a teacher who is able to guide them into and through the truth. It is in this function that the teacher learns to lead by influence and not merely by authority, and it is to this kind of teaching that teenagers best respond. Guiding means allowing youth to make mistakes and being there to help them work through difficult situations.

Facilitator

A dynamic teacher is also a facilitator. Facilitators are teachers who enable their students to help themselves. Once again, they resist the temptation to simply deliver information. They do not do all the work for the students nor do they supply all the answers. Rather, they create an environment and atmosphere through which the Holy Spirit can move so that opportunities for growth are always present.

Motivator

Teenagers often show up in Sunday School classes or Bible studies without any particular sense of purpose. Perhaps their parents made them come; maybe they like someone in the class; or perhaps they simply have nothing else to do. At any rate, they need some serious help in finding a reason for learning. One of the rather difficult tasks of the youth teacher is to motivate otherwise unmotivated teenagers to get excited about learning and applying God's Word.

Counselor

While youth workers are generally not professional counselors and are not usually equipped to do crisis or clinical counseling, teachers will be called upon from time to time to assist teenagers in working through their problems. Teachers are often not aware that this role will be thrust upon them. However, teachers of youth who are open, available, good listeners, and who genuinely care for their students will find that informal counseling naturally occurs. In your role as teacher, expect to counsel young people on issues such as parent/

teen relationships, dating and marriage, career, peer pressure, peer relationships, and school. For more life-threatening issues such as suicide, eating disorders, drug and alcohol abuse, and sexual or physical abuse, referral to professional counselors is required.

Mentor

Youth teachers assume the role of mentors as some of their students desire assistance in developing a deeper walk with Christ. In this role, teachers may become personal guides or tutors. This can often bring with it greater demands and expectations on the teacher as the students' dedication increases. But of all roles, this might be the most special. It calls for being more like the Master Teacher—not only in teaching and character but also in guiding others to become disciples who, in turn, become mentors of others.

Resource Provider

Lucien Coleman likens the teacher to a broker. In the business and commercial world there are people who sell certain commodities and others who want to buy the commodities. Prospective buyers and sellers, however, are not always aware of one another, and it becomes the task of the broker to serve as a go-between for those buying and those selling.[5]

Similarly, a teacher's task is to bring learners and resources together. The well-equipped teacher knows what resources are available to the student of the Bible and is able to direct students to such items as concordances, commentaries, Bible dictionaries and encyclopedias, related computer programs, maps, topical Bibles, and books on biblical topics and relevant issues.

The Spiritual Gift of Teaching

One of the spiritual gifts mentioned in three of the New Testament passages dealing with spiritual gifts is teaching (Rom. 12:7; 1 Cor. 12:28-29; Eph. 4:11). All Christians will have some responsibility to teach others as they grow in their faith. But those with the spiritual gift of teaching will be endowed by the Holy Spirit with the special ability to discover and communicate facts and insights from Scripture to others in ways in which they can learn and apply them to their lives.[6]

How do you know if you have the gift of teaching? This gift may be discovered by asking a few questions of yourself:[7]

1. *Is it something to which I am drawn? Do I like doing it? Do I enjoy watching those who do it well? Do I find myself searching out ways to become a more effective teacher?*

2. *Do I see myself improving and developing in skill the more I teach?*
3. *Are my initial fears about teaching being replaced with a growing sense of competence?*
4. *Do others recognize the gift in me?*
5. *Are the lives of youth benefiting spiritually as a result of my teaching?*

All too often, youth classes are filled simply out of a desperate need for workers. Rather than simply trying to fill teaching positions with willing bodies, Sunday School and youth ministry leaders should endeavor to do the best they can in recruiting and equipping for the classroom those believers who have been empowered by the Holy Spirit with the gift of teaching.

Conclusion

Every teacher is to aspire to the goal of the ideal, and a teacher of youth is no exception. The characteristics required of the effective youth teacher are framed around the needs of adolescents—a close relationship with Christ, a love for youth, a knowledge of the Word, an understanding of teenagers, and an ability and giftedness in the area of teaching. The teacher of youth will also fill a number of roles—model, guide, facilitator, motivator, counselor, discipler, and resource provider. These are great demands to be placed upon any teacher, but the greater challenge is to forge a lifestyle that demonstrates God's power and guidance in every aspect of living—for it is through teachers that teenagers see the reality of Christ in action.

For Further Discussion

1. What would you say as evidence to combat Carl Roger's statement that teaching is a relatively unimportant activity?
2. Think of the teachers who have impacted your life the most. What primary roles did they play? What role/s generally typify you as a teacher?
3. Do you have the gift of teaching? Take time to answer the five questions offered in the text to find out.

Notes

1. C. V. Eavey, *Principles of Teaching for Christian Teachers,* 19.
2. Reginald W. Bibby and Donald C. Posterski, *Teen Trends,* 320.
3. Herman Harrell Horne, *The Teaching Techniques of Jesus,* 143.
4. Lois E. LeBar, *Education That is Christian,* 173-74.
5. Lucien Coleman, *Why the Church Must Teach,* 111.
6. Ray C. Stedman, *Body Life* (Glendale, CA: Regal, 1972), 42-43.
7. Ibid., 54-55.

Understanding Youth as Learners

4

It goes without saying that knowing and understanding youth as learners is absolutely critical to having a successful teaching ministry with them. However, since learning, like teaching, is such a common and universal experience, it is easy to overlook or ignore the complexities of how students learn. This chapter is designed to help teachers discover some of the critical elements of how youth learn.

Biblical Understanding of Man

Disciplines such as science, psychology, developmental psychology, and sociology can provide much information about the adolescent as a learner, but these disciplines alone do not give us the complete picture. To fully understand adolescents as learners we must understand them theologically as well as scientifically.

The Handiwork of God (Ps. 8)

"What is man?" writes the psalmist David in one of his hymns. The response to the query comes quickly and assuredly: "You made him a little lower than the heavenly beings and crowned him with glory and honor" (Ps. 8:5). We are God's handiwork, created beings of the Almighty God.

To confess that we are the product of God's handiwork entails realizing three assumptions: 1) that we are dependent on God, 2) that we find our origin in God alone, and 3) that we have a special purpose in life. These truths are important for teens to know as they search for a sense of identity, self-worth, and meaning for life.

Image of God (Gen. 1:27)

Not only are we God's wonderful handiwork, but we are also created in His image (Gen. 1:27). While theologians debate the notion of the *imago dei* (or image of God), there is some accord as to what it means. One of the aspects of *imago dei* is the capability to reason. Unlike other creatures, humans have the ability to contemplate the nature of life and to know the Creator Himself.

A second element of the *imago dei* is the capacity for relationship and fellowship. Because of this capacity, humans have the ability to communicate and relate to themselves, others, God, and even the natural world.

Teachers must consider these aspects of the image of God when they plan for educational experiences. Since teenagers possess the capacity to think and reason about God, issues, and life itself, effective teaching must utilize this God-given intellectual potential. Teachers must also seek to help youth become involved with other people (teenagers as well as adults) so they might grow with and from them, since ultimately the notion of fellowship or community implies a shared experience. Finally, teachers must develop the teenage learner's ability to communicate with self, others, and God.

Sin and Consequences (Gen. 3:1-24)

We are God's handiwork, created in His image, but there is a dark side of human nature the Bible calls *sin*. Although this view of human nature runs contrary to contemporary educational approaches, an accurate understanding of Christian teaching necessitates a serious examination of sin and its consequences. Genesis chapter 3 offers a detailed account of how sin entered the world. It informs us that the human race began its existence in perfect innocence and harmony, but through a single act of disobedience, it fell. This cycle of disobedience has continued on in every generation and in each individual life. What is sin? Sin is simply "missing the mark" or failing to live up to what God desires for us. It is so pervasive that the Bible says everyone sins (Rom. 3:23) and that "everyone who sins is a slave to sin" (John 8:34).

Christian education of teenagers must address the realities of sin and its debilitating consequences in the following ways:

•❖ by assisting teens in personally acknowledging the reality of sin;

•❖ by helping to bring youths' lives into closer harmony and fellowship with God and others through reconciliation;

•❖ by assisting teenagers into gaining freedom from the enslavement of sin;

•❖ by recognizing the role of evangelism in the education of youth.

Necessity of Conversion (Rom. 6:23)

One of the consequences of the fall and sin is alienation from the Creator. But while the wages or consequences of sin is eternal separation from God, the Good News is "eternal life in Christ Jesus" (Rom. 6:23b). Christian education of youth must include the basic truths of biblical faith, which include the saving acts of God through the birth, life, death, and resurrection of Jesus Christ. Furthermore, a constant emphasis upon personal response to Christ and the need for commitment must be placed before teens.[1]

Domains of Learning

Educators and educational psychologists generally recognize that learning takes place in three distinct areas or domains: cognitive, behavioral, and affective. The cognitive domain is the intellectual dimension of an individual and embodies knowledge acquisition, information processes, and thinking skills. The affective domain includes intangible elements such as the emotions, attitudes, and values. The behavioral domain relates primarily to actions and lifestyle. For young people to experience holistic faith development or spiritual formation, the learning experience must include a balanced emphasis on each of the domains of learning. Accentuating one domain at the expense of the other two can lead to distorted development. For example, an emphasis on the cognitive dimension can lead to a spiritually dry intellectualism; an unwholesome focus on behavior can bring with it legalism or Pharisaism; and a concentration on only the affective can foster emotionalism.

Cognitive: Knowing and Understanding

Cognitive learning is that which we typically associate with the primary purposes of formal education—the acquisition of facts and the assimilation of new information. For example, students might endeavor to discover truths in a particular portion of Scripture, to study the various positions on the return of Christ, or to receive information on the consequences of pre-marital sex.

Content-oriented teaching will be comprised of several major elements: guidance in following Jesus, knowledge and practical application of Scripture, a proper concept of who God is and how to worship Him, critical reflection on every aspect of life.[2]

While knowledge about God and His Word is important, knowing about God must never be confused with knowing God. James reminded his readers that even the demons know about God but do not truly know Him (James 2:18-19). Regrettably, too many Christians (including ministers, youth pastors, theology professors, etc.)

have a sound intellectual grasp of theology and the Scriptures but lack a dynamic relationship with God.

Affective: Feelings, Attitudes and Values

A second domain of learning is the affective. While the affective domain is the most difficult to teach for and perhaps the most neglected, it is nonetheless an essential dimension of learning and faith development. It refers to the conviction or passion a person has about the knowledge he or she posesses. While the cognitive is linked to the head, the affective is linked to the heart and embraces or internalizes what one believes with the head. To ignore the affective domain of a youth's Christian education is to risk nurturing a relationship with God lacking passion, warmth, and personalization.

While learning related to the intellect usually takes place in the formal classroom setting, teaching for affect is often done best in informal settings such as a wilderness trip. Classroom techniques that are helpful in cultivating affective change include simulation activities, drama, role play, case studies, and music.

Behavior: Doing

The Christian faith is more than simply knowing or feeling. The crowning aspect of one's faith is the ability to live out in obedience that which is believed (the cognitive) and valued (the affective). Jesus refers to this dimension of the Christian walk when He says, "If you love me you will obey what I command" (John 14:15). James declares, "Show me your faith without deeds, and I will show you my faith by what I do" (James 2:18). Effective teaching of youth must include teaching them to make wise and well thought-out lifestyle choices.

Ways of Learning

Everyone who teaches youth makes certain assumptions about how they learn. Teachers may not be able to clearly articulate a theory of learning; nonetheless, the teaching strategies and techniques they employ are based on some considerations as to how their students will learn best. There are three major families of contemporary learning theory; however, to explore these families to much extent would go beyond the perimeters of this book.[3] A few of the more prominent theories helpful for the teacher of youth are highlighted here.

Reinforcement Learning

Some educational theorists explain human behavior and learning primarily in terms of environmental stimuli. The most popular of these theories is B.F. Skinner's theory of *operant conditioning,* which argues that those behaviors (*operants*) that are positively reinforced (*conditioned*) are more likely to be repeated. A *reinforcer* is any reward or positive event that follows an action. The learning assumption here is that if a teacher rewards a behavior, the student will probably repeat it, and conversely, if a teacher ignores or punishes a behavior, it is less likely to be repeated. Effective classroom reinforcers can be divided into three categories: 1) *social* reinforcers (acceptance, hugs, attention, smiles); 2) *symbolic* reinforcers (prizes, points, grades); and 3) *activity* reinforcers (games, music, trips).[4]

Although there is truth to this theory, the behavioristic approach has some weaknesses in light of Christianity. First, the Christian walk entails much more than right behavior. Christian education of youth is concerned with holistic change—internal commitment as well as external conduct. The danger of reinforcement learning exists in altering the observable external behavior without changing the heart attitude.

Second, although the notion of learning reinforcement exists in Scripture (the Bible is replete with situations where God promises blessings for good behavior and curses for disobedience), if reward is the only motivation for young people to obey and serve God, it becomes inappropriate and reflects an immature faith. Reinforcement techniques that are most appropriate for teenagers are those that encourage and reassure, such as verbal expressions of praise, approval, and encouragement.

Learning Through Modeling and Imitation

According to Albert Bandura, a significant amount of acceptable human behavior is learned from imitating and observing the actions of others.[5] The old adage "Like father, like son" illustrates the impact observational learning has in the home. But this principle of learning applies to other learning environments as well and is well-illustrated in Scripture. The Apostle Paul instructs the Christians in Corinth by saying, "Follow my example, as I follow the example of Christ" (1 Cor. 11:1), and Jesus advises that "everyone who is fully trained will be like his teacher" (Luke 6:40).

Klaus Issler and Ronald Habermas delineate two types of modeling—*structured* and *spontaneous.*[6] The explicit purpose of *structured modeling* is to intentionally demonstrate how to perform a particular function or act. For example, a youth pastor who desires to teach one of his teenagers how to evangelize might take him along when he shares his faith with a friend.

Spontaneous modeling, on the other hand, is not planned—it simply happens. It is the youth worker living his or her life before youth.

C. Doug Bryan describes the powerful impact this kind of modeling can have on youth. He says, "No other factor can produce greater harm than an unworthy model; no other factor can produce greater benefit than a worthy one. Individuals will emulate or follow the life demonstrated before them."[7]

Discovery Learning

An approach to education that appeals to the cognitive processes is Jerome Bruner's *discovery learning.* Bruner maintains that students should not be presented with information or material in its final form; rather, they should be encouraged to discover facts and information relationships individually or in groups.

While proponents of discovery learning agree students will learn fewer facts through this approach, they argue they will gain a deeper understanding of the subject matter that will carry them beyond the classroom. Another strength of this approach is it teaches youth to do independent and critical thinking. Students must be equipped to use the information they receive in class to reflect personally on situations, events, and problems.

Although the discovery approach has many strengths, it also has some drawbacks. First, discovery methods can be too time consuming. Teachers may feel precious class time is being wasted while students discover truths and concepts that could be more quickly learned with a simple teacher-centered explanation. Second, the discovery learning method may be inappropriate in some settings, especially if the subject matter is too difficult or if students come from disadvantaged backgrounds. Discovery methods are also less effective with students who are unmotivated, less confident, or slow in learning.

Teachers can incorporate discovery learning into the classroom by using open-ended questions, debates, case studies, and dilemmas. In employing discovery methods in classes for Christian youth, the following suggestions are offered:[8]

✓ *Emphasize contrast* (e.g., contrast the free will of man with the sovereignty of God);

✓ *Stimulate and encourage informal guessing* (e.g., allow students to imagine or explore possibilities as to what heaven might be like, and follow up by looking at portions of Scripture that describe heaven);

✓ *Encourage participation* (e.g., engage students in a variety of active learning experiences and games);

✓ *Allow students to solve problems on their own* (e.g., break the class into small groups or triads to answer open-ended questions related to a portion of Scripture with the help of Bible study aids);

✓ *Arouse curiosity* (e.g., use "hooks" or attention grabbers such as video clips, songs or song lyrics, skits, etc. to introduce the issues or relevant Scripture passages);

✓ *Introduce disturbing or contrasting data* (e.g., ask students to read a book, go on a field trip, or watch a video that confronts them with facts contrary to what they have previously believed);

✓ *Allow students to make mistakes.*

Experiential Learning

"Experience is the best teacher!" This is a proverb often quoted to emphasize that ultimately we learn best by doing. America's leading educator and philosopher in the first half of the twentieth century was John Dewey, who insisted that all genuine education comes through experience. While Dewey has been no friend to evangelical Christianity, his focus on the student's experience is worthy of consideration.

Does the learner's experience have a significant place in the discipleship process? Certainly Jesus used the experiences of His learners for instruction. His training of the Twelve clearly combined instruction, modeling, and experience. For example, Luke 9 recounts how Jesus called the Twelve together, instructed them on how to preach the Kingdom of God, gave them authority to drive out demons and to heal the sick, and then sent them out to do the work of ministry. This account was followed by the feeding of the five thousand, where the disciples assisted Christ in ministering to the masses. This was yet another opportunity for the disciples to receive on-the-job training for ministry!

D. James Kennedy is well known for his success in equipping lay people to witness. In his book *Evangelism Explosion,* he relates the following account: "Finally it struck me like a bolt of lightning—I had taken classes for three years and had not learned how to witness. It was not until someone who knew how had taken me out into people's homes that I finally got the confidence to do it myself. Thus I began the program . . . . It began by taking out one individual until he had confidence to witness to others, and then another and then another."[9] Through observation and experience, students of Dr. Kennedy simply followed the pattern Jesus had set for training His own disciples.

Some performance-oriented tasks can only be learned by doing. A baseball player can receive only so much instruction on how to hit, field, or pitch. At some point he must go out and practice these skills himself. In the Christian walk, some beliefs or spiritual lessons are best learned by experience, and often the lessons of life are held more dearly than the lessons of formal education.[10]

Memory Learning

Anyone working with youth wants his or her students to remember what they learn so they will be able to transfer what they learn to a number of situations. Proponents of *information processing learning* are concerned, among other things, with how the memory works and with the ways learners can improve their memory capability.

A number of techniques can be employed to strengthen memory skills.

Rehearsal. One of the most common ways to learn chunks of information is to repeat it, either verbally or silently, over and over.

Clustering. Clustering is reorganizing material into more meaningful subgroups. For example, the Ten Commandments can be organized into two clusters: one cluster including commands related to God Himself and a second cluster including commands related to others.

Meaningfulness. Learning is meaningful to the extent that new concepts can be related to the existing knowledge of the learner. Teachers can help youth make connections between new information and prior knowledge by using metaphors, analogies, and examples. Jesus demonstrated this when he used sheep and goats to describe two types of character (Matt. 25:31-46). Since His listeners clearly understood the differences between sheep and goats, they were able to firmly grasp Jesus' meaning. In the same way, our teaching will be more effective when we use familiar illustrations with our students.

Mnemonic Devices. Mnemonic devices are little jingles or phrases that help us recall information. There are different types of mnemonic devices. For instance, an example of a rhyme mnemonic would be "Columbus sailed the ocean blue in fourteen hundred and ninety-two." Another type of mnemonic is the acronym. An example of this would be using the first letters from the Great Lakes—Huron, Ontario, Michigan, Erie, and Superior—to spell the word HOMES. Acrostic is a third type, which involves making up a sentence where each word begins with the to-be-learned item. An example of this type of mnemonic, used to help learn lines on a music staff, is Every Good Boy Does Fine.

Learning Styles

Based on personality and past learning experiences, each student has developed preferences as to how he or she likes to learn. In a Sunday School class or in other educational settings, students learn best when the teaching style matches their preferred learning style.

A number of learning style theories have been developed to help educators appeal to a variety of learning preferences. One popular model, developed by Bernice McCarthy, has been effectively adapted for Christian education by Marlene LeFever.[11] While no individual teenager will fit one of the four styles perfectly, most teenagers will feel that one out of the following foursome fits them best.

Imaginative Learner. Imaginative learners are feelings-oriented youth who enjoy getting involved with others and learn most effectively in settings that nurture interpersonal relationships. These students learn best by listening and sharing ideas, as well as sensing, feeling, and watching. They tend to see the big picture more easily than the small details.

Analytic Learner. These students learn primarily by watching and listening. They expect the teacher to be the primary information giver while they sit and carefully analyze and assess the content received. Their emphasis is on facts, logical ideas, and an organized presentation of information. They will prefer traditional teaching methods such as the lecture and be uncomfortable with teachers who try to be innovative and creative in their teaching styles.

Common Sense Learner. Common sense learners like to test ideas and theory in real-life situations. They excel in educational settings that deal with subject matter that is practical and of immediate relevance to them. They learn best by doing; thus, teaching techniques that are experiential in nature are most appealing to them.

Dynamic Learner. Dynamic learners also enjoy hands-on learning, but rather than thinking through ideas logically, they like to follow hunches and sense new directions and possibilities. These creative learners appreciate flexibility and change and find joy in discovering something new or in "putting their personal stamp of originality on an idea."[12]

How can the teacher of youth teach to all four learning styles? It is clearly impossible to develop lesson plans that appeal to each individual learner. However, the four styles provide a framework for working with learning and teaching techniques. An individual lesson or entire curriculum can be designed in such a manner that it features as many learning modes as possible. It is suggested also that optimum learning occurs when students are encouraged or challenged to employ all learning styles—not just the one they prefer to use.

Conclusion

A necessary assignment for the teacher of youth is to understand youth as learners. The first step in this process is gaining a biblical understanding of man. The second step is to become familiar with many of the prominent approaches to learning: reinforcement, modeling and imitation, discovery, experience, and memory techniques. Though educational theorists disagree on how students learn, and they explain learning in a variety of ways, teachers can still gain valuable insights from them that are helpful for teaching. An awareness and application of learning styles will also enable the teacher to be more effective in the classroom.

For Further Discussion

1. Why is it critical to start out with a biblical understanding of man when seeking to understand youth as learners?
2. What are the results of a focus on only the cognitive domain of learning? How might one teach for the other domains?
3. Why do teachers often hesitate to allow students to engage in discovery learning? What are its benefits?
4. Name a spiritual truth you learned experientially.
5. Think of two or three people in your family and try to identify their learning styles. How would you plan a lesson for them?

Notes

1. Robert W. Pazmino, *Foundational Issues in Christian Education,* 2d ed. (Grand Rapids, Mich.: Baker, 1997), 57.
2. Jim Wilhoit, *Christian Education and the Search for Meaning,* 109-10.
3. The three major families of contemporary learning theory are the conditioning theories (which emphasize behavior change), information-process theories (which emphasize the learner's intellect), and social learning theories (which accentuate modeling). See Klaus Issler and Ronald Habermas, *How We Learn,* and Perry G. Downs, *Teaching For Spiritual Growth,* for an excellent approach to learning theory from a biblical perspective.
4. William R. Yount, *Created to Learn,* 165-66.
5. Albert Bandura, *Social Learning Theory* (Englewood Cliffs, NJ: Prentice-Hall, 1977.
6. Issler and Habermas, *How We Learn,* 83-84.
7. C. Doug Bryan, *Learning to Teach, Teaching to Learn,* 44.
8. Yount, 203-4, 226-27; Robert F. Biehler and Jack Snowman, *Psychology Applied to Teaching,* 354, 426-34.
9. D. James Kennedy, *Evangelism Explosion,* 4th ed. (Wheaton, Ill.: Tyndale, 1970), 9.
10. For helpful insights on learning by experience from a biblical perspective see Downs, *Teaching For Spiritual Growth,* 183-95.
11. Marlene D. LeFever, *Learning Styles* (Colorado Springs: David C. Cook, 1995).
12. Ibid., 21.

Creating a Climate for Learning

5

Learning is a dynamic, albeit delicate, relationship between the student and his or her surroundings. The motivation to learn, and indeed learning itself, is influenced and enhanced to a great extent by external factors. Effective teachers know how to motivate youth to learn and how to create an environment that promotes learning; ineffective teachers do not. There are at least four ways the teacher of youth can maximize learning through the creating of a dynamic classroom climate: 1) by establishing meaningful teacher-learner relationships, 2) by exhibiting positive personality factors, 3) by employing instructional behaviors that enhance the emotional climate, and 4) by structuring a positive physical environment.

Motivating Youth to Learn

Why is it some youth in your class seem eager and ready to learn, while others appear unmotivated and resistant to anything you have to offer? The effective and conscientious teacher will be sensitive to the readiness of a student's responsiveness to the class.

The following list offers some suggestions on why some youth lack motivation to learn:
- ✓ the subject is boring;
- ✓ the subject matter is presented in a boring way;
- ✓ the student would rather not exert him/herself;
- ✓ the student does not know what to do;
- ✓ the student lacks ability or aptitude;
- ✓ parents are not encouraging about the experience;
- ✓ the student has had negative experiences with learning;

33

✓ the student feels insecure or afraid;
✓ the student feels a lack of acceptance and belonging;
✓ the student has a low level of aspiration.

One of the overall reasons a lack of motivation pervades a learning environment is that the youth teacher has not strategically planned for motivation. There are several strategies a teacher can employ to counter most of the barriers to motivation mentioned above.

Arouse curiosity and interest. Topics such as prayer, devotions, servanthood, or faith do not always jump out to teenagers as exciting or interesting. However, if the teacher can convince the youth these topics are what they need or should be interested in, motivation to learn can be increased. One way teachers can arouse curiosity and interest is by creating "cognitive dissonance" in the minds of the students. When beliefs or ideas are out of harmony, motivation is activated to resolve the dissonance. For example, a teacher can create dissonance in a class by asking students to explain how the concepts of man's free will and God's sovereignty can co-exist in Scripture. Humor, storytelling, captivating problem-based scenarios, challenging assumptions, and provocative questions are some additional ways to arouse curiosity.

Use reinforcement effectively. While external rewards work well for young children, educators have come to learn that extrinsic motivation can actually decrease student interest among adolescents. Even so, one extrinsic reinforcer that can still be effective is praise. Praise that is credible and sincere and given in moderation gives the student feedback on performance and provides a sense of worth.

Create a warm emotional climate. It is important to know that positive attitudes about the learning environment are also strong motivational factors. Students must know they will not be embarrassed or humiliated in any way. For example, do not require students to read aloud (perhaps they are poor readers or cannot read) and always assure students that wrong answers are okay. Demonstrate an interest in your students by learning and using their names, allowing students to share interesting experiences, or sending notes or cards to students who miss class.

Make learning relevant. If teens do not perceive the lessons presented to them as relevant or meaningful, they will likely remain aloof and uninvolved. Teachers can better know the felt needs, interests, and passions of their students through an assortment of needs assessment techniques (e.g., interviews, questionnaires, inventories). In the classroom, the teacher must introduce meaningful content and exercises, learn to find common ground with youth, and become adept at making contact with students' needs and interests.

Instill confidence. Youth are motivated when they are confident of their success in learning new material and performing new tasks. A teacher can build confidence in his or her students by letting them know when they are making progress, by providing learning opportunities where they can experience success, by making expectations clear, and by assigning challenging but not overwhelming tasks.

Satisfy expectations. Satisfaction occurs in a learning situation when student expectations are met. For intrinsically (or inwardly) motivated youth, it is important that they be able to use new knowledge or skills in a meaningful way. Extrinsically motivated teenagers will be satisfied when their learning results in an anticipated reward.

Teacher-Learner Relationships

In addition to knowing the basics of motivating youth to learn, there are several external factors that greatly affect learning. In his book *Teacher Effectiveness Training,* Thomas Gordon declares there is one factor that stands above all else as the difference between teaching that fails and teaching that works and brings rewards. That factor is the degree of effectiveness the teacher has in establishing quality and meaningful relationships with students.[1] In fact, many of us have probably heard it said that the three key principles to effective youth ministry are *relationships, relationships,* and *relationships.* Although the Holy Spirit is always the most critical ingredient in teaching, the importance of relationships with youth cannot be stressed enough. Jesus serves as an ideal model for us here as we see Him developing close, intimate relationships with His disciples as a context for His teaching.

What does this mean practically for the youth teacher? How can the teacher of youth nurture warm and healthy relationships with class members? Here are a few prescriptions.[2]

Maintain a love for youth. Above all, the teacher must have a love for youth. All youth must be accepted, welcomed, and loved.

Listen with understanding. The youth teacher needs to befriend youth and then to be willing to counsel and listen with understanding to the problems or issues they are facing.

Know the youth. The teacher should get to know youth personally and as individuals. This requires time spent in one-on-one or small group situations outside the classroom context. It also involves getting to know youth through visitation in their homes, social activities, various personal encounters, and personal contacts made with youth on their own turf.

Be involved. The teacher must be willing to be involved in the lives of students. By being transparent, caring, fair, and impartial, the teacher will enhance the possibility of youth coming to him or her to talk about their problems.

Earn the right to be heard. Finally, youth teachers must realize the right to be heard is earned through the way they treat youth. Youth will be more likely to give a teacher a fair hearing if they have seen the teacher's compassion and concern actively demonstrated to them in the past.

Teacher Personality and Learning Climate

Youth ministry classrooms, like most educational settings, are intricate and complex arenas in which a variety of emotional reactions can significantly affect learning and student participation. Perhaps the safest generalization to make about emotions in regards to learning is that any emotion described as pleasant is usually conducive to learning. Conversely, we can assume that negative emotions such as fear, rejection, and incompetence are disruptive to learner motivation. More specifically, teachers who are effective in the classroom nurture learning by exhibiting positive personality factors.[3]

Warmth and acceptance. Youth teachers who are warm, loving, and caring create a positive emotional tone in the classroom and encourage learning and participation.

Enthusiasm. Enthusiasm refers to the great excitement or interest the teacher generates towards the subject matter. Teachers with enthusiasm are contagious. By contrast, teachers who appear consumed with their notes, who move methodically and monotonously through the lesson, or who demonstrate little excitement over the whole classroom experience pass on this lack of enthusiasm to their students. Apparently, Jesus taught with such intensity and enthusiasm that "the crowds were amazed at His teaching" (Matt. 7:28).

Teaching flexibility. Teaching flexibility refers to the willingness to use variety in methods and techniques according to the classroom needs. Such teachers tend to be more positive and democratic than other more rigid teachers. Rigid teachers are those who tend to use the same strategies repeatedly, regardless of student outcomes. Flexible teachers focus on the learners and use whatever means are most helpful in ensuring that transformation of the learner takes place.

Emotional maturity. Emotionally mature teachers are characterized by a sense of humor, a pleasant manner, a sense of justice and fairness, and a disciplined lifestyle. Immature teachers are prone to be unpleasant, impulsive, easily irritated, indiscreet, anxious, and short-tempered. Immature teachers can make the learning experience extremely unpleasant, if not unbearable, for students.

Teaching Behaviors and Positive Emotional Climate

The emotional climate of a classroom refers to the degree of tension and/or harmony felt by members of the class and is reflected in the cohesiveness of the group. Teachers can help create positive emotional climates not only by building meaningful relationships and exhibiting positive personality factors but by employing certain teaching behaviors that are conducive to group cohesion. While the following strategies are drawn from theory and research in adult education, they will be clearly helpful in fostering a positive climate for youth education.

Create a learner-centered environment. In a learner-centered classroom the teacher's behavior and learning activities will reflect a concern for the particular needs of each youth. The teacher will take into consideration the personal interests of students, demonstrate a conviction as to the worth of each individual, and concentrate on individual spiritual development. Creating a learner-centered environment also means giving precedence to meeting the needs of youth over the accomplishment of tasks when these two values come into conflict.

Nurture a high level of trust and openness. Teenagers may often find it difficult to share information, ideas, thoughts, feelings, or reactions to the lesson being taught. However, if they sense that a high level of trust exists in the class, they will be more willing to discuss and disclose information. As the teacher, you can motivate youth to be more open by sharing your personal testimony, including the struggles, victories, and defeats you have experienced in life.

Encourage a spirit of freedom. Do members of the class sense a freedom to express their opinions and thoughts without being ridiculed or censured? Adolescents can sometimes be critical or arrogant towards those who think differently than they do. However, the freedom to express one's honest views is absolutely essential for creating a positive emotional climate for learning.

Provide a spirit of authority. A corresponding spirit of authority must temper freedom of thought in youth classes. Adolescent learners must know there is sufficient authority in the class to demonstrate that their quest for spiritual development and Christian truth is a serious and critical undertaking.[4]

Facilitate group communication. One sign of group cohesiveness is an ease and ability to talk and listen attentively to one another. By fostering group interaction, young people are given the opportunity to connect interpersonally with each other and to learn to respect the thoughts and opinions of others.

Foster a spirit of cooperativeness. Cooperation overrides competition as a strategy for establishing a warm emotional learning climate. Teenagers should be encouraged to achieve their best, but this is not done by putting them in a winning or losing position with their peers. While self-chosen competition may be appropriate on the playing field, it is less valuable for fellow learners when it occurs in a classroom setting and can be the source of much anxiety and poor self-esteem.

Encourage an acceptance of personal responsibility. When teenagers hold themselves accountable for their individual choices and behaviors, they are less likely to blame others or make excuses for the consequences of their self-chosen actions.

Establish clear and accepted learning outcomes. When learning goals are clearly defined, accepted, and desired by youth, it is more likely that they will cooperate and be motivated toward proper behavior.

The Physical Environment and Learning

There is one more body of information the youth teacher must pay close attention to in nurturing a healthy climate for learning and spiritual formation—the physical environment. While the physical environment is not necessarily determinative in creating a positive learning climate, the surroundings can go a long way in influencing the emotional climate. For instance, Jesus generally did not teach in a formal classroom setting; instead, he used the natural environment to maximize His pedagogical effectiveness. For example, He used the mountainside as a natural amphitheater (Matt. 5:1); He employed objects as visual aids (Matt. 6:25-31, 21:18-22; Mark 12:13-17); and He used a boat as a prop for teaching.

The physical environment consists of four elements: 1) the learning room, 2) teaching tools, 3) the natural environment, and 4) learning mediums.

The Learning Room

What message is sent to youth about learning as they enter the classroom? Is the room arranged with the teacher's chair or podium at the front with the rest of the chairs placed in straight rows, signifying a traditional approach to the teaching-learning process? Or are the chairs placed in a circle, indicating a more interactive, student-centered strategy? Is the room uninviting—poorly lit, cluttered, dirty, drab? Or does it present itself as a place where youth would want to hang out? These are the kinds of questions the perceptive teacher might ask when assessing the learning room itself.

To make the learning setting functional and inviting, special attention and care must be given to such features as floors, walls, room and class size, and room and chair arrangements. For instance, the larger the classes, the less likely youth are to interact. The structure of the chairs, for example, will determine such aspects as visibility and the ability to hear, the formality or informality of the class, the degree to which all members will be involved in discussion, and the group dynamics that will take place.

Teaching Tools

Teaching tools are physical objects a teacher uses to enhance teaching and improve student learning, better known as visual or audiovisual aids. These aids enhance teaching by appealing to different styles of learning. They also are helpful in generating interest in the subject matter. For example, an alarming video on the dangers of sex before marriage will get students talking much faster than a simple verbal introduction to the topic. Finally, these tools can sometimes present the message visually in a way words cannot.

There are a number of tools that may enhance one's teaching of youth: dry erase boards, flip charts, overhead projectors and transparencies, handouts, charts and graphs, maps, props, videos, and PowerPoint™ slides. Although the benefits of visual aids are many, one must always remember that teaching tools are designed to supplement the teacher as the presenter, not to replace him or her.

The Natural Environment

Although formal learning situations generally take place indoors, there are still certain elements of the natural environment that affect teaching and learning.

Time of day. The time of day a class or small group meets affects participation and interest. Students may be more awake for a class after ten in the morning than before. If a small group meets in the evening, it is likely some teens will be tired from the days' activities.

Day or night of the week. The particular day or evening of the week a class meets may not affect learning or classroom participation, but it may affect attendance. With so many contemporary youth holding down part-time jobs, close attention should be paid to finding the best time for classes or small groups to meet.

Lighting. Classrooms should be installed with ceiling lights that give adequate, even lighting. Attention should be given to outside, natural light as well. Occasionally, sunlight reflections or glares can be a distraction or make it difficult to see. Be sure the room has adequate blinds to keep out unwanted sunlight and that it is possible to darken the room for video or slide presentations.

Noise. Nothing can detract from effective teaching and learning like external noise. Take whatever precautionary and reactionary measures necessary to cut down the possibility of outside noise disturbing your teaching.

Temperature. The temperature of the room is a significant factor in how well adolescents are able to concentrate, listen, or interact. Since temperature preference is an individual matter, encourage youth to wear layered clothing in order to adjust to the room temperature.

Learning Mediums

Learning mediums differ from teaching tools in that while tools are designed to help the teacher present the message, mediums are intended to set the mood or to help prepare youth for the learning experience. For example, flowers serve as a nice touch when placed on the registration table at a conference. For youth classes, the following learning mediums might be appropriate: music, name tags, food or drink, and posters.

Conclusion

Motivating youth to learn and creating an emotional climate and physical environment that maximizes learning enjoyment, participation, and success is indispensable to dynamic teaching. As a teacher, you must never rely on student motivation alone; instead, you must take steps to strategically plan for motivation. Additionally, as you go about the task of teaching for life change, you must look at several factors including teacher-learner relationships, teacher personality, emotional climate, and physical environment and ask yourself the question, "What can I do in these areas to create an environment that enhances the learning experience for teenagers?"

For Further Discussion

1. Have you ever experienced a class where students were extremely motivated to learn? What made the difference?
2. Do you agree relationships are the most important aspect of teaching? If so, why is this often hard to live out?
3. Name persons in your church or ministry who demonstrate each of the positive personality factors of a teacher.
4. Why is group cohesion so important to the classroom?
5. Evaluate your ministry in regards to the physical environment.

Notes

1. Thomas Gordon, *Teacher Effectiveness Training*, 2.
2. John M. Dettoni, *Introduction to Youth Ministry*, 48-49.
3. Summarized from Yount, *Created to Learn*, 296-98.
4. Findley B. Edge, *Teaching for Results*, 40-41.

Understanding Adolescents:
Developmental Characteristics

6

Adolescence, especially the early years (roughly ages twelve to sixteen), is a period of dynamic growth impelling the teenager towards adulthood. Rapid and dramatic changes occur in a number of developmental areas: physical, cognitive, emotional, personal identity, social, moral, and faith. Consequently, adolescence is an extremely difficult and tumultuous period of life. An understanding and awareness of these developmental changes can help the youth teacher understand teenagers and some of the issues and crises they are encountering.

Physical Development

The physical change that early adolescents experience is phenomenal and second only to the marvelous metamorphosis that takes place in infancy. Adolescence is generally thought to begin with puberty, the process whereby a child is biologically and sexually transformed into an adult.

The initial noticeable anatomical changes in boys at puberty are the growth of testicles and penis enlargement (around age eleven). For boys, major changes in puberty also include growth spurts in height and weight, growth of axillary (underarm, and facial hair) and pubic hair, and the development of sweat glands (giving rise to body odor). Additional changes include voice deepening, the onset of acne and other skin eruptions, and an increase in muscular strength. On the average, most boys have their first spontaneous ejaculation (often in the form of a wet dream) at about age thirteen. Teenage boys usually finish developing physically at about age sixteen or seventeen.

41

For girls, the onset of puberty is marked by the initial menarche or menstruation (usually occurring somewhere between the ages of ten and sixteen, with the highest frequency at about age thirteen), along with the appearance of pubic hair and the development of breasts. As girls continue to grow, their breasts develop further and the shape and curvature of their hips change. Like the boys, girls also experience a physical growth spurt, the growth of axillary hair, and an increase in sweat gland activity.

Until early adolescence, boys and girls are equal in physical strength and development. Around the ages of twelve or thirteen, girls may even have a strength advantage over boys their age and are able to compete with boys in athletics. After the completion of puberty, however, physical changes will not only make a girl look more feminine, they will place her at a physical disadvantage to most boys. After the pubertal growth spurt, a boy's muscles, heart, and lungs are larger and his body has a greater capacity than the female's for carrying oxygen to the blood.

In these years of turbulent and rapid change, teenagers desperately need affirmation in their physical and sexual identity. The adolescent tasks of achieving identity, establishing self-worth, and gaining peer acceptance are all related to the acceptance of one's body and sexuality. Biological and sexual development can be the source of much consternation and confusion for both boys and girls. Boys and girls who are early or late in development experience different perceptions and attitudes towards self and reactions from peers. Youth workers are challenged to be sensitive to the wide variety of developments represented in any youth group. They must also explain to young people that while sexuality is a special gift from God to be enjoyed in the appropriate way, it must not be abused or exploited.

Intellectual Development

Paralleling the dramatic biological changes that are unfurled in the early adolescent years are the equally notable changes that occur in the intellectual or cognitive domain. During the childhood years, thinking ability is connected primarily to the manipulation of concrete facts and observations. Around the ages of eleven or twelve, however, young people make a transition to what developmentalist Jean Piaget calls *formal thinking* skills. Formal or abstract thinking is characterized by the ability to do the following: think about possibilities, think about hypotheses, think about the future, think about self, and anticipate the thoughts of others.

First, the formal thinker can now think in terms of *possibilities.* Adolescents become adept at manipulating abstract ideas and imagining all sorts of possible situations, even those they have never encountered. Consequently, they can imagine the ideal society, church, family, and/or parents and compare the imagined states of perfection with the imperfect reality that surrounds them. The result is often severe criticism of those people and institutions that often do not measure up to the imagined ideal. This can lead to a critical and argumentative spirit as teens seek to create cases for their positions.

The adolescent can also think through *hypotheses,* or in terms of "if this . . . then this" patterns. Thus, while younger children may solve problems by the trial and error method, maturing teenagers become more adept at plotting a course of action and testing hypotheses or possible solutions. They can imagine alternatives, anticipate consequences of possible choices, and systematically reason themselves through problems or difficult situations.

Abstract thinking skills also enable adolescents to *think ahead.* This ability, along with the capacity to imagine possibilities and solve problems, extends them the competency to make decisions regarding school and choice of classes, to consider vocational and career possibilities, and in other ways, to reason and plan for the future. This newly-discovered cognitive skill, however, can at times be the source of frustration and confusion. For example, since the adolescent can anticipate the consequences of taking on a particular job, he or she may feel threatened or intimidated enough to postpone the choice.

During early adolescence, young people develop the ability to *reflect on themselves.* Because their bodies, feelings, and intellectual powers are undergoing such dramatic change, they tend to be preoccupied with their own beings. They also perceive themselves in a rather critical or negative manner. David Elkind suggests teenagers make a characteristically critical error at this point. When they think about other people's thinking, they assume others are thinking about what they are—themselves! They then proceed to construct what he calls an *imaginary audience* that they believe is constantly watching them and evaluating their behavior. This imaginary audience, he adds, accounts for the self-consciousness that is so characteristic of the early adolescent.[1]

Being sensitive to certain aspects of adolescent thinking can help the youth teacher respond with patience and graciousness. For example, the teacher might be a little more understanding of the tendency for teenagers to be overly critical of the church and society. Teachers should also take advantage of teens' increased reasoning powers by addressing doctrinal and ethical issues and introducing abstract theological concepts. Now is also the opportune time to move away from an emphasis on storytelling and information-giving strategies to include teaching techniques that encourage independent and critical thinking. In settings that promote thinking, students are coached and encouraged to question, ponder, imagine, and solve complex problems.

Identity Development

One of the major challenges of adolescence is self-discovery, the task of what the late Erik Erikson and other psychologists term *identity formation*. A sense of identity is not innate or inborn. Rather, says Elkind, "It is an active construction that results from an ongoing effort to integrate and make sense of our experience as it pertains to ourselves."[2] During the formative years of adolescence, young people engage in the process of discovering how they fit into society and the roles they will eventually play in life. Identity formation includes the evaluation and reflection on the goals, values, and beliefs teens have inherited from family, peers, church, and other elements of society. It necessitates the asking of personally reflective questions such as "Who am I ?" "Where did I come from?" and "Where am I going?" It also involves a number of other factors which include forming a self-esteem; establishing personal autonomy; belonging to a group of peers; struggling through issues of sexual identity, development, and gender roles; and making decisions related to life-planning and personal faith. The imposing task of adolescence is to pull all of this disparate and sometimes confusing information together in a cohesive manner that helps the youth make meaning out of life and provides a sense of knowing who he or she is. It is increasingly important that youth teachers are a support and encouragement during this crucial time.

Identity Types

Expanding on the foundational works of Erikson, James Marcia proposes four identity types or statuses of adolescents: *identity diffused, identity moratorium, identity foreclosed,* and *identity achieved.* Each status describes where a teenager might be in regards to his or her identity formation. According to Marcia, two criteria are necessary for mature identity achievement: *crisis* and *commitment.* Crisis refers to the struggle or emotional turmoil a teenager goes through in making choices; commitment describes the amount of personal investment an individual exhibits in making a choice. These are important to identity because without some sort of crisis or deep soul searching in making important life decisions there is question as to whether a decision is really one's own. Similarly, without a strong commitment to life choices, there is the possibility one has not weighed the full rewards and costs of these choices and will most likely abandon them as soon as opposition or difficult circumstances arise.

Identity-diffused. These youth are characterized by a lack of crisis and personal commitment in terms of goals, values, or beliefs. This type of youth has no real sense of identity and tends to be confused, withdrawn, and out of place. To put off the responsibilities of making commitments and important decisions, this youth may engage in intense, immediate experiences such as parties, drugs, and thrills to provide a "right-now" sensation. Often these teens' fathers are absent through separation or divorce, and those fathers who are home may be detached and unencouraging.

Identity-foreclosed. Foreclosed teenagers are those who have expressed commitment to a particular set of goals, values, and beliefs but have never had the corresponding crisis to go with it. These youth can tell others what they want in life or what they believe, but they have never grappled with issues of personal identity. They have never struggled through the questions of what it is they feel called to be and do or how God has gifted them uniquely; rather, they assume a commitment that is handed down to them by others, particularly their parents. For example, this is the student who decides to be a doctor because it is what everyone in the family has always done. Foreclosed youth are well-behaved, cooperative, and submissive to authority—they tend not to be troublesome. Unfortunately, these young people also remain cautious and overly dependent on others and are unlikely to provide creative leadership or direction. These youth may have parents who are possessive and overly intrusive with their children.

Identity-moratorium. Youth who are in moratorium are rather vague about commitments but are in the midst of weighing out possibilities and are actively struggling with alternatives. This is the teenager who is going to be an astronaut one day and a missionary the next. The youth worker must realize these are not flippant choices, but rather, seriously considered options. The moratorium stage might be considered the most normal approach to adolescent identity-seeking. This is because the culture tends to treat the whole decade of adolescence as a moratorium during which the teenager gradually assumes more and more adult responsibilities and characteristics yet without the full accountability that accompanies adulthood. Youth teachers can assist these teenagers by giving them the space and encouragement to explore and search for answers to the options and possibilities that confront them.

Identity-achieved. These youth have not only grappled with issues that matter but have settled personal commitments that contribute to an integrated, well-developed sense of identity. They have considered, for example, a number of occupational options and have come to decisions on their own terms, even though their ultimate decisions may be a variation of the desires of their parents. In regards to their faith, they have re-evaluated past beliefs and have achieved a resolution whereby they have internalized and taken ownership of these beliefs and values. In general, these adolescents have by and large achieved identity and are ready to assume the roles and responsibilities that adulthood brings. They will also most likely emerge as key leaders in their youth groups and should be encouraged into such ministry opportunities as leading small groups, organizing service projects, and helping plan and carry out youth programs.

Moral Development

How do individuals make moral and ethical decisions?[3] How do children, youth, and adults react when placed in situations that involve deceit, generosity, love, and self-control? These questions related to moral reasoning challenged Lawrence Kohlberg to formulate his scheme of moral development.

Kohlberg proposes that we move through three levels (each divided into two stages) of moral reasoning. The first level, *preconventional* (so called because children do not understand the conventions of society), characterizes the reasoning of pre-adolescents. At this level, children are preoccupied with the physical consequences of an action or with the benefits that might be derived from right behavior.

In adolescence, however, there is a shift towards *conventional* morality (Kohlberg's level 2), which is moral reasoning that is influenced more by others than by the consequences of behavior. At the first stage in this level (stage 3), acceptable behavior is that which is approved by others; thus, peer pressure plays a critical role in adolescent reasoning. Behavior is also judged more by its intentions than by its impending consequences. Thus, a high-school girl can easily overlook the inappropriate actions of the star quarterback who cheated on his exams so he would not be kicked off the team. Her response might well be, "He did it for the good of the team!"

At stage 4, the maturing teenager adopts a "law and order" mentality. According to this approach, rules of conduct in society must be established and obeyed without question. Rules continue to be given from the outside, and conflicts between youth and their parents will emerge as teens experience discrepancies between the values of peers or society and their parents. The sensitive teacher of youth will notice that teenagers are often legalistic and simplistic in their value system although their actions or behavior may not always correlate with their stated beliefs and values.

As teens grow older (ages thirteen to young adult), they move to Kohlberg's level 3, *postconventional.* In this level, students are beginning to make independent moral decisions. Rather than looking to others or to the conventions of society, they are making moral choices based on a concern for the legitimate rights of the individual (stage 5) and a concern for ethical principles (stage 6). It is at this level of moral development that youth teachers can present a biblical code of ethics to teens and encourage them in the process of making wise, well-reasoned moral choices.

Faith Development

One of the critical tasks in the nurturing and discipling of Christian teenagers is to enable them to come to the point where they appropriate or internalize their faith. In other words, youth teachers want to see their students develop a firsthand faith.

What is faith? From a theological perspective, faith is the response of the individual to the redemptive work of the Holy Spirit in his or her heart. This response includes all dimensions of one's personhood: the intellect (an acknowledgment of certain truths), emotion (a heartfelt response of love to God), and volition (the will to act upon and respond to that which is believed).[4] Knowing this, what should we as teachers expect from our teens in terms of faith development? How much can we expect from them in terms of obedience to God, heart conviction, and personal commitment? To help us answer these questions, we turn to theories of faith development.

The seminal work on faith development is James Fowler's *Stages of Faith.* Fowler suggests people go through stages of faith development just as they go through stages of cognitive or moral development. As young people move into their early adolescent years (approximately age twelve and on), they move into what Fowler calls *synthetic-conventional* faith. It is synthetic in the sense that it is non-analytical, coming as sort of a unified, global whole. It is conventional in that it is being shaped by or conforming to the beliefs and values of significant others. That is, it reflects the faith system of the entire community. Note that though there may be a deep emotional involvement or attachment to values and beliefs on behalf of the young teen, the authority resides primarily outside the self, in significant others (parents, youth workers, and the church). Furthermore, it exists relatively unexamined. It is a *second-hand* faith. John Westerhoff calls this faith *affiliative,* characterized by a strong sense of belonging and a need for the interaction of significant others.[5]

The next stage of faith, according to Fowler, is the *individuative-reflective*, and may begin to emerge in late adolescence. This type of faith is individuative in the sense that it is one's own; it is reflective in that the individual has taken the time and mental energy to examine and critically think through what he or she believes. It is to this kind of firsthand faith we want to bring our teens.

With the development of a teenager's intellectual skills and the accompanying ability to internalize one's faith, at least two suggestions for the youth teacher bear mentioning. First, the teacher should welcome difficult questions of the faith and remind students that it is not wrong to have doubts about their faith. Second, teachers should nurture a firsthand faith by providing opportunities for students to reflect individually on their faith. More about this will be said in a future chapter.

Conclusion

Adolescence is a dynamic period of development, and it marks a special time in God's plan for life change. These years can be the source of turbulence, frustration, and pain; they can also be filled with joy and gratification. As adolescents experience the trauma of biological metamorphosis, learn to think and reason on a new level, shape their identity, make moral choices, and begin to internalize their faith, teachers of youth will play a significant role in nurturing them toward maturity and propelling them into the next stage of life—young adulthood.

For Further Discussion

1. When have you seen intellectual growth in the youth you have known? How can Bible teachers harness these new skills?
2. Identify young people from the Bible who may have been experiencing the various statuses of identity formation. (For example, David, Daniel, Moses, Samson, Jacob, Esau, etc.)
3. What words would you use to describe a teen's moral choices?

Notes

1. David Elkind, *A Sympathetic Understanding of the Child,* 211.
2. Ibid., 196.
3. For a great teaching resource on making ethical choices, see James P. Eckman, *Christian Ethics in a Postmodern World* (Wheaton, Ill.: Evangelical Training Association, 1999).
4. Stanley J. Grenz, *Created for Community,* 19.
5. John Westerhoff, *Will Our Children Have Faith?* 94.

Understanding Adolescents:
Youth Culture

7

The previous chapter discussed the internal forces impacting the adolescent experience. But there is another body of information the youth teacher must pay close attention to—youth culture. It is the interplay between these two forces (biological conditions and social/cultural environment) that shapes the profiles of adolescents. Teaching and working with adolescents requires that we have a sound theology of culture as well as an understanding of the adolescent world.

Youth Subculture Analysis

In a sense, any attempt to capture a snapshot of current youth culture is an exercise in futility, since contemporary culture changes at a breathtaking speed. Because youth culture is constantly in such a state of fluctuation and metamorphosis, a book or any portion of a book on youth culture or subcultures would become antiquated in a relatively short period of time.

Yet we would be amiss if we disregarded the study of youth culture or skipped over it altogether. In fact, the Church in general and even many youth teachers are pitifully oblivious to various elements of the youth subculture and mistakenly ignore what is occurring among adolescents at large. Furthermore, most teachers do not have any semblance of a clear, well thought-out theology of culture. They have not taken the time to contemplate on how the Christian should view culture in light of biblical teaching. This "head in the sand" approach to culture in general, and more specifically youth culture, has led to a pursuit of youth ministry that misses the mark in understanding the culture-laden issues and circumstances that are confronting youth today.

Reasons for Cultural Analysis

With these thoughts in mind, the following list provides a few reasons why it is crucial for the youth teacher to carefully analyze and understand youth culture:

☛ so the youth teacher can keep pace with a constant and rapidly changing teen culture;

☛ so the youth teacher can gain a better understanding of adolescents and the issues they are facing;

☛ so the youth teacher can identify and better minister to the specific needs of adolescents today;

☛ so the teacher of teens can understand the beliefs, presuppositions, and values represented in contemporary youth culture;

☛ so the youth worker can better understand the interplay between internal struggles and external influences that together shape the lives of adolescents;

☛ so the youth worker can assist adolescents in bringing their faith to bear on the world in which they live.

Dangers of Cultural Analysis

While there is tremendous value in analyzing youth culture, there are some definite dangers involved. Some of these are listed here.

✓ *The danger of over-generalization:* thinking in terms of the "average" teenager. No such individual exists—every youth is, in a sense, unique.

✓ *The danger of paralysis by analysis:* exerting too much effort exploring culture, at the expense of being students of the Word.

✓ *The danger of secularization:* placing trust in one's ability to critically analyze and problem solve, while forgetting that ultimately God is the change agent.

✓ *The danger of the "razor's edge":* living so close to the culture one is analyzing that one loses the power to view it objectively. In order to fully understand a culture, one must view it with fresh eyes.

✓ *The danger of neutrality thinking:* sometimes in endeavoring to be open-minded in studying culture, Christians lean towards a neutral or non-ethical stance. This is dangerous because it can lead to compromise and diminish one's ability to be salt and light to a sinful world.

What is Youth Culture?

Is there a youth culture or subculture that is distinct from the dominant culture? The observant visitor to the local mall or typical U.S. high school will recognize that not only is there a youth subculture, but there is what Anthony Campolo calls a "kaleidoscope of subcultures."[1] A wide variety of youth subcultures exist alongside of each other—preppies, druggies, skaters, jocks, Christians, nerds, and granolas, to name just a few. Each of these subcultures has its own set of values, interests, and characteristics, along with its own worldview and language. The general youth subculture can then be further divided along ethnic, geographical, and class lines. Unfortunately, there is often a great temptation to treat all youth as if they belonged to a single, identifiable subculture. Campolo goes on to say that "it is easier to design programs and curriculum for ministry if we yield to that temptation. Sweeping generalizations about young people's needs, psychology, and beliefs provide us with an imagined cultural mind-set for which we can develop 'relevant' ministries."[2]

We must remember that the most relevant ministries are the ones that understand youth for exactly who they are. Being wary of broad, generalizing stereotypes of youth culture, we must take the time to learn about the different groupings and personalities of youth that exist within our own spheres of ministry. Understanding teenagers and their world is not easy, and teaching youth who are a part of one particular subculture will require techniques, psychological understanding, and a linguistic approach that will be unique and distinctly different from any other subcultural group.

Elements of Youth Subculture

Youth teachers work with youth in the context of their subcultures. Their television programs, music, fads and styles, and lingo are all designed to distinguish them from the dominant adult culture. Hans Sebald proposes a number of dimensions or basic elements of a youth subculture that serve to fulfill that function.[3]

Relatively unique norms and values. Teenagers hold to *norms* (rules concerning how to achieve values and do certain things) and *values* (attitudes concerning what is important) that are, if not entirely different from the adult community, reflect a unique emphasis. Some standards relate to popularity, prestige, friendship, and sex.

Teen lingo. Teen subcultures often have an *argot* or special language unique to the members of that particular group. Teen lingo serves a number of functions. It enhances group cohesiveness, serves as a precise reference to unique teenage experiences, reflects what is important to a particular subculture, and functions as a prestige gauge among peers.

Distinct channels of communication. Subcultures need special channels of communication in order to maintain a sense of solidarity or unity. The simplest channel of communication exists in the form of person-to-person interaction that takes place, for instance, on the high school campus. However, subcultures also need mass communication to help solidify the subcultural norms, and mass media helps to accomplish this. The Internet, television, movies, home videos, MTV, radio, teen magazines, song lyrics, and advertising all bombard the teenage population with values and ideas that become uniquely adolescent property.

Unique fads and styles. A fad is a relatively new way of doing, speaking, grooming, or dressing. Fads serve as status measurements, allowing teenagers an opportunity to achieve prestige in the eyes of their peers by conforming and excelling to particular observances in vogue.

A sense of solidarity. Solidarity or *esprit de corps* refers to a sense of belonging that pervades with feelings of closeness and intimacy. Teenage solidarity is often reflected in teens' attempts to exclude adults from their activities and styles.

Hero worship. Most subcultures come equipped with leaders. Yet when we observe the broader North American teen subculture, we note that for the most part, leadership is conspicuously absent. Instead, there is sort of a hero orientation whereby teenagers "worship" or exhibit special adoration for individuals in the entertainment world: rock musicians, athletes, and movie and television actors. The worship of these heroes is often observed in overt demonstrations such as cheering wildly at concerts, posting pictures of heroes on bedroom walls, and imitating popular idols in dress and hairstyles.

Subcultural institutionalization. The overall function of the youth subculture is to provide compensation for the failure or neglect of the adult or dominant culture to provide a sense of identity, status, acceptance, and need-satisfaction unique to adolescents. If the dominant culture fails to provide an institutional framework for the gratification of certain needs, the youth subculture may develop one to fulfill the need. Examples of youth institutions are dating, music festivals, dancing, drug use, and music.

Christ and Culture

When teaching and working with teenagers in the context of culture, we struggle with the tension that exists between our Christian faith and the broader culture. How do we view the relationship between Christ and culture? How are we to be the salt of the earth and the light of the world and to become all things to all men on one hand, yet keep ourselves from being polluted by the world on the other? How are youth encouraged to celebrate their cultural identity without succumbing to the anti-Christian passions of the world? How do youth teachers and ministers do youth ministry in the context of the subculture while maintaining a distinctly Christian approach? The classic paradigm for assessing a Christian's attitude towards culture is provided by the theologian H. Richard Niebuhr. He identifies at least four ways to view the relationship between Christ and culture.[4]

Christ against culture. According to this view, the world is so hopelessly corrupt that the only option one has as a Christian is to separate oneself from it. Adherents of this position may cite Paul's warning to the Corinthians to "come out from them [unbelievers] and be separate" (2 Cor. 6:17) and James' injunction to "keep oneself from being polluted by the world" (James 1:27). Youth ministry that reflects this approach will plan programs that compete with the activities of the world, such as Christian dances and even sporting events. Teaching tends to be authoritarian in nature and difficult questions and doubts often go unanswered. The weakness of the isolationist approach to ministry is that Christian youth will not know how to relate to the broader culture and will have relatively little impact on society.

Christ of culture. In sharp contrast to the "Christ against culture" approach is the "Christ of culture" one. This model is much more optimistic about the world and eagerly embraces many of the cultural norms and latest trends. In this approach to youth ministry, confrontation of culture is rare, and programs will be quick to emulate whatever is popular within the youth culture at large. While there may be a sincere attempt to be relevant, youth ministries of this nature often focus on entertainment and numbers. Those who are in this camp might point to the example of Christ who "came eating and drinking" and was a friend of tax collectors and sinners (Luke 7:34).

Christ above culture. This approach to faith and culture divides the sacred and secular into two distinct compartments that rarely, if ever, intersect. This duelist approach suggests that what happens on Sunday or at youth group meetings has relatively little to do with what occurs during the rest of the week. Students learn indirectly that their faith lacks relevance to life and has little bearing on daily choices.

Christ transforming culture. According to this model, one recognizes that culture is tainted and in need of transformation but does not shy away from engaging in it. Proponents of this view will work through the tension of being in the world but not of it. The youth teacher will be interested in every facet of teens' lives and equip them to be change agents in a needy world. Youth will be effectively taught as to how to bring their faith to bear on culture and society.

Doug Stevens suggests the following implications for the teacher who operates from the "Christ transforming culture" approach:[5]

1. Each and every one of us is a part of culture—we have our roots in it; we are influenced by it; and we are called to remain in it.
2. We need to become conversant with the youth culture as it is.
3. We must carefully evaluate the elements of youth culture.
4. We must become comfortable in culture—enjoying it, participating in it, and relating to it.
5. We must, however, paradoxically remain ever restless. We are sojourners in this world, and we must acknowledge that Christ transcends every cultural norm.

Conclusion

Perhaps the most difficult task for many adult youth teachers is keeping conversant and up-to-date on the world in which their students live and find their roots. However, in an effort to make the timeless message of the Gospel relevant to a generation of youth that are shaped by a particular set of values, beliefs, trends, and worldviews, careful analysis of youth culture is not an option. Furthermore, it is the role of youth workers to enable the youths themselves to bring their faith to bear on a world desperately in need of transformation.

For Further Discussion

1. Why is the "head in the sand" approach to youth culture unacceptable for the Christian teacher?
2. In your opinion, what is the most compelling reason for cultural analysis? What is the greatest danger?
3. How is youth culture today different from the culture when you were growing up? What are some reasons for the changes?
4. Can you name any lingo, fads, or heroes unique to teens today?
4. Describe the tension between the Christian faith and culture.
5. How can a knowledge of youth culture aid in teaching?

Notes

1. Anthony Campolo, "The Youth Culture in Sociological Perspective," in *The Complete Book of Youth Ministry*, 37-47.
2. Ibid., 37.
3. Hans Sebald, *Adolescence*, 226-277. See also James A. Davies, "Adolescent Subculture," in *Handbook of Youth Ministry*, ed. Donald Ratcliff and James A. Davies (Birmingham, Ala.: Religious Education Press, 1991), 7-41.
4. H. Richard Niebuhr, *Christ and Culture* (New York: Harper & Row, 1951). See also Dean Borgman, *When Kumbaya is Not Enough* (Peabody, Mass.: Hendrickson, 1997), 7-83, and Doug Stevens, *Called to Care*, 93-97, for applications of Niebuhr's paradigm to youth ministry.
5. Stevens, *Called To Care*, 95.

Understanding Adolescents:
Critical Issues

Today's youth are part of a troubled generation—a generation, some suggest, at extreme risk. While psychologists and youth workers have long characterized the adolescent years as a difficult and tumultuous stage of life, those who currently observe and work with adolescents are concerned about the extreme difficulty many young people face in navigating the highways of life. Each generation of youth seems to face an increasingly complex, stressful, and threatening world. This chapter examines the statistics and trends observed as one millenium moves into the other.

Ideally, the teenagers sitting in church pews and attending Sunday School classes would be somehow immune from the dangers that are plaguing the larger youth population. Of course this is not true. Many churched teens are struggling under the sometimes unbearable hurts and pains that life affords. Others are engaged in one or more at-risk behaviors. This chapter represents the darker side of adolescence and youth ministry—the critical issues confronting today's teens.[1]

Family Problems

Of the various institutions and groups to which teenagers belong, the family is undoubtedly the most significant in shaping their lives. While the family is designed to provide security, affection, emotional support, and protection from a sometimes unfriendly and hostile world, many youth come from homes characterized by conflict and dysfunction. The contemporary family is ravaged by divorce and separation, father absenteeism, and numerous other problems. Many (probably the majority) of teenagers sitting in our Sunday School classes and other youth ministry programs are from homes of distressing family situations.

Divorce and Separation

Divorce is more common today than at any other point in the history of the United States. It can be stated with a certain amount of assurance that two out of every five marriages today will terminate in separation or divorce affecting an enormous number of teenagers.[2] The effects on teenagers are devastating and long-lasting. In a monumental long-term study on the impact of divorce on children and teenagers, Judy Wallerstein and Sandra Blakeslee found widespread experiences of rejection, intense loneliness, and guilt in the lives of children and adolescents of divorced families.[3] Merton Strommen discovered that youth who come from homes of divorce or separation are bothered by lack of family unity, have lower estimates of self-worth, have more difficulties in school, and demonstrate a lower interest in religious matters.[4]

Dysfunctional Families

In addition to divorce, there are numerous other family configurations that are dysfunctional in nature. These family situations are likely to put teenagers in stressful predicaments and may lead to a variety of at-risk behaviors.

Single-parent Families. In the United States, over 25 percent of children under the age of eighteen live in a single-parent home,[5] and estimates of the probability that a young person will live with only one parent at some time before reaching the age of eighteen are as high as 60 percent.[6] Research has demonstrated that living in a single-parent home can be harmful, even destructive. For example, a study by the Search Institute revealed that adolescents from single-parent families were consistently more likely to be engaged in at-risk behaviors (such as binge drinking, school absenteeism, suicide attempt, theft, fighting) than those from intact two-parent families.[7]

Blended Families. Blended or reconstituted families are those in which one or both of the remarried partners bring at least one child into the new family relationship. One study revealed that more adolescents from blended families evidenced deviant behavior, erotic activities, parent-youth conflict, and identity achievement problems than those from nuclear families (those families with both natural parents and children in tact).[8]

Latchkey Families. Latchkey families are those in which the parents are not available to their children before or after school or on holidays. Latchkey children are so named because they often wear a house key on a string or chain around their neck to let themselves into their homes after school. On any given weekday in the U.S. and Canada between the hours of 3:00 P.M. and 6:00 P.M., millions of children and teenagers are in their homes without adult supervision. The detrimental effects of latchkey experiences on children and adolescents include high incidences of loneliness, fear, stress, and conflict; increased use of drugs and alcohol; unsupervised television viewing; increased sexual activity; risk of safety; and difficulties in school.[9]

Family Violence and Conflict. Merton Strommen insists that the most decisive variable in identifying hurting youth is exhibited when parents are at odds with each other. On the other hand, one of the predictors of greater unity in the family is the extent of parental accord. Sadly, Strommen reports only half of the population of church youth report harmonious accord between their parents.[10]

Father Absenteeism. In most cases, father absenteeism occurs as a result of divorce or separation. However, even with intact families, many fathers are absent because they spend relatively little time with the family. The reasons for this are many: fathers may be preoccupied with career or self-fulfillment or lacking in the ability to establish emotional closeness with the family. Thus, in many homes, parenting is primarily the task of the mother.

Child Abusing Families. One of the real tragedies of today's youth is abuse. Child abuse occurs in a number of forms: sexual abuse, physical abuse, verbal and emotional abuse, and parental neglect. Sexual abuse is any form of sexual behavior with a child including fondling, exhibitionism, incest, and rape. Physical abuse includes acts such as slapping, punching, or kicking. Emotional and verbal abuse occurs when teenage children are subjected to ridicule, harsh criticism, withholding of affection, or irrational punishment. Neglect happens when parents fail to safeguard the health, safety, and well-being of their children.[11] Unfortunately, rates for family abuse, date rape, and sexual abuse of children by other children (especially teens) indicate an upswing in occurrences.

Substance Use and Addiction

The consumption of alcohol and drugs by today's youth creates a tremendous burden on them. Concerns of youth workers and parents over substance use and abuse are not unfounded as American youth begin smoking, consuming alcohol, and taking drugs in preteen or early teen years. Reports indicate that the United States has the highest incidence of teenage substance use among industrialized nations.[12]

Alcohol

Drinking among adolescents, especially older teens, is almost a universal phenomenon and serves as a rite of passage from childhood to adulthood even though it is illegal in the U.S. for anyone under the age of twenty-one to purchase alcoholic beverages. It is indeed the drug of choice for North American teenagers. According to a report to the Surgeon General, 68 percent of all students have consumed alcohol at least once and eight million or 38.6 percent of all students drink weekly.[13] For teens who attend church, the rates may be lower, but not all that reassuring to parents and youth workers. According to a Search Institute study, half of church-attending adolescents used alcohol in the last year. A staggering 69 percent of the juniors and seniors tasted alcohol at least once in the past year.[14]

Christian parents of teens are at times relieved to find their child is "only drinking." Research indicates, however, that drinking and driving remains the number one killer of teens, that alcohol consumption is strongly related to criminal and promiscuous behavior, and that alcohol is the leading gateway drug to heavier drug use.[15]

Illicit Drugs

Almost all teenagers in the United States and Canada are exposed to illicit drugs, and a large percentage of youth either experiment with them or are addicted to them. While teenage drug use declined since peaking in the 1980s, it appears that it is on the rise again.[16] Forty-one percent of high school seniors have tried an illegal drug and 25 percent have used an illicit drug other than marijuana.[17]

How do the habits of church youth compare to those of the general youth population? The Search Institute found that 20 percent of the juniors and seniors in their study of church youth admitted to using marijuana in the past year and 3 percent had tried cocaine.[18] Teenage drug use is one of the most perplexing, dangerous, and challenging problems facing society today, and statistics clearly indicate that many cherished youth fall prey to the lure of this deadly habit.

Tobacco and Smokeless Tobacco

Despite the well-advertised health risks associated with smoking, sizable numbers of teenagers are still establishing cigarette habits. Cigarettes have been tried by nearly half of eighth grade students, and at least 17 percent of high school seniors are smoking on a daily basis. Among male eighth graders, 34 percent have tried smokeless tobacco, although only 4.3 percent of seniors use it on a daily basis.[19]

Eating Disorders[20]

Virtually unheard of in the first half of the twentieth century, the diagnosed incidences of eating disorders have been increasing at a staggering rate. As many as 25 percent of today's teenagers, mostly girls, are affected by either anorexia or bulimia nervosa.

The better known, though less common, of the eating disorders is *anorexia nervosa,* which literally means "nervous loss of appetite." Anorexia is essentially a self-inflicted starvation whereby the individual compulsively refrains from eating in order to attain thinness. The anorexic teenager usually suffers from physical side effects such as intolerance to the cold, excessive skin dryness, low blood pressure, heart problems, chemical deficiencies, depression, social withdrawal, insomnia, and irritability. About 2 percent of the total population suffers from this disorder (over 90 percent of whom are adolescent females).

Closely related to anorexia is *bulimia nervosa,* which literally means "ox-hunger." This eating disorder is characterized by binge eating followed by purging through self-induced vomiting, laxatives, exercise, and/or fasting. Bulimics are generally healthier than anorexics, although side effects may include menstrual problems, dental problems, and depression. Approximately 19 percent of female teenagers are bulimic.

It is difficult to understand why certain teenagers would subject themselves to behaviors that are so destructive to the body and soul. However, researchers have identified three common cultural or societal factors: 1) individuals with eating disorders are overwhelmingly female; 2) the onset for either disorder usually occurs in the late teens; and 3) those with disorders come almost exclusively from middle and upper socioeconomic classes.[21] In addition, experts have identified several reasons that precipitate the onset of eating disorders: perfectionism, low self-esteem, identity problems, family pressures, social pressures, and the influence of the media.[22]

Teenage Sexuality

Teenagers today are growing up in a sex-saturated culture. Unfortunately, the messages communicated to them from television, movies, advertising, the Internet, magazines, and music are contrary to values built on biblical foundations. Tragically, churched youth are also succumbing to the pressures of a society that is sex crazed.

Premarital Sexual Intercourse

For many of today's youth, sexual intercourse is no longer seen as a moral issue or an activity reserved for marriage only. According to a national school-based survey of the Centers for Disease Control (CDC), a huge 76 percent of boys and 67 percent of girls in the United States have experienced sexual intercourse by age eighteen.[23] The rates for churched youth are much lower but still of concern. Josh McDowell and Bob Hostetler discovered that 27 percent of the churched teens in their survey had engaged in sexual intercourse by age eighteen. In other words, the young people sitting in your Sunday School class have over a one-in-four chance of engaging in sexual intercourse by the time they graduate from high school![24]

Teen Pregnancy

One of the critical issues of teenage sexual activity is teenage pregnancy. The United States is in the midst of a teenage pregnancy epidemic unrivaled by any other industrialized nation. Every day, close to 3,000 girls become pregnant, approximately one million a year. Almost half of these pregnancies end in abortion.[25]

Sexually Transmitted Diseases

Premarital sexuality brings with it the possibility of contracting one or more sexually transmitted diseases (STDs). Around three million American teenagers contract STDs annually—more than any other age group in the United States.[26] Of course the most devastating STD is AIDS, the deadly disease caused by the HIV virus. It is estimated that each year 40,000 teenagers contract the HIV virus.[27]

Adolescent Homosexuality

For a small percentage of adolescents, the sexual experience includes homosexual acts or feelings. While youth workers may feel ill at ease and inadequate in addressing homosexuality, it is possible that some adolescents in their classes or groups are struggling with this issue. Homosexuals may constitute as much as 10 percent of the total youth population. For those young people who claim to be homosexual, the consequences can be devastating. Not only are they at greater risk for contracting the HIV virus than heterosexual youth, but they are up to three times more likely to try to kill themselves.[28] Many gay and lesbian youth, afraid to let friends, parents, teachers, or youth workers know of their orientation, lead painfully lonely and isolated lives.

Violence at School

Violence is becoming increasingly prevalent in the United States, and it is spreading into the public schools. Each year from July 1994 to June 1998, approximately 45 violent incidents resulting in deaths occurred in school-associated settings.[29] Although the recent news reports of school shootings are making the public more aware of the problem of school violence, it is still true that the vast majority of schools are safe places (with less than one percent of all homicides and suicides among school-aged children occurring in or around school grounds or on the way to or from school).[30] Nevertheless, protective fences, metal detectors, locker searches, student shake-downs, and uniformed security officers are not uncommon sights in many big city public schools and suburban schoolyards that often resemble battlegrounds rather than centers of learning.

Adolescent Suicide

At an escalating rate, young people are choosing to take their own lives in response to the overwhelming struggles and pressures they are facing. In the USA, the rate of suicide for adolescents aged fifteen to nineteen has quadrupled since 1950.[31] Suicide is one of the leading causes of death in the youth population with anywhere between 4,000 to 6,000 teenagers taking their lives annually. In their study of churched youth, Roehlkepartain and Benson discovered that 40 percent of the adolescents surveyed had contemplated suicide at least once during the previous twelve months.[32]

Conclusion

This chapter may have reflected a dim view of the world of contemporary youth. Granted, many youth—including churched youth—engage in at-risk behaviors or are anxious over critical issues. But there is a positive side. For example, the Youth Risk Behavior Surveillance System (Centers for Disease Control) studied trends of risk behavior from 1991 to 1999 and found that the prevalence of several injury-related and sexual behaviors have improved among U.S. high school students. At the end of the decade, fewer students were at risk for motor-vehicle crashes, homicide, unintended pregnancy, and STDs (including HIV infection) than at the beginning of the decade.[33] In addition, Barna Research Group found that almost six out of ten teens say they are satisfied with their family situation.[34] Merton Strommen points to the significant number of youth whose "joy is in a sense of identity and mission that centers in the person of Jesus Christ."[35] Finally, George Barna reveals that almost half of our teenagers have volunteered at least some of their free time to help needy people.[36] Let us address the critical issues teens are facing, but let us not forget to build on the strong convictions and zeal that characterize many youth.

For Further Discussion

1. Why do we often refuse to believe that youth in our churches or ministries are facing the same critical issues and at-risk behaviors as the larger youth population?
2. What were the most surprising statistics to you in the chapter, if any?
3. What issues or behaviors have you recognized most frequently among teenagers you have known?
4. Which critical issue or behavior do you feel most unprepared to handle? How might you become more prepared?
5. Pick an issue or at-risk behavior from the chapter and outline a possible church response.

Notes

1. For a more extensive treatment of these issues and behaviors see Harley Atkinson, *Ministry With Youth in Crisis.* Also see the Instructor's Guide for this course for suggestions in handling these issues and organizations which can help.
2. Charles Sell, *Family Ministry* (Grand Rapids, Mich.: Zondervan, 1995), 42.
3. Judy Wallerstein and Sandra Blakeslee, *Second Chances* (New York: Ticknor and Fields, 1989), xii.
4. Merton Strommen, *Five Cries of Youth,* 44.
5. U.S. Bureau of the Census, *Statistical Abstract of the United States, 1996,* 116th ed. (Washington, D.C.: GPO, 1996), 65.
6. J. Jeffries McWhirter et al., *At-Risk Youth: A Comprehensive Response,* 42.
7. Peter L. Benson and Eugene C. Roehlkepartain, *Youth in Single-Parent Families,* 17.
8. A Search Institute study cited by Strommen, 65.
9. Frances Smardo Dowd, *Latchkey Children in the Library and Community* (Phoenix, Ariz.: Oryx Press, 1991), 13-18.
10. Strommen, 53-54.
11. McWhirter et al., 42.
12. Myra Pollock Sadker and David Miller Sadker, *Teachers, Schools, and Society,* 4th ed. (New York: McGraw-Hill, 1997), 494.
13. US Department of Education, *Youth & Alcohol: Selected Reports to the Surgeon General* (Washington, D.C.: GPO, 1993), 11.
14. Roehlkepartain and Benson, *Youth in Protestant Churches,* 100-101.
15. U.S. Department of Education, *Youth & Alcohol: Selected Reports to the Surgeon General,* 14-29.
16. Sadker and Sadker, 494.
17. Lloyd D. Johnston, Patrick M. O'Malley, and Jerald G. Bachman, *National Survey Results on Drug Use, 1975-1992,* vol. I (Rockville, Md.: National Institute on Drug Abuse, 1993), 19.
18. Roehlkepartain and Benson, *Youth in Protestant Churches,* 100-101.
19. Johnston, O'Malley, and Bachman, 19.
20. Summarized from Atkinson, *Ministry With Youth in Crisis,* 212-19 and Les Parrott III, *Helping the Struggling Adolescent,* 105-18.

21. Denise E. Wilfley and Judith Rodin, "Cultural Influences on Eating Disorders," in *Eating Disorders and Obesity*, ed. Kelly D. Brownell and Christopher G. Fairburn (New York: Guilford Press, 1995), 78-82, and L.K. George Hsu, *Eating Disorders* (New York: Guilford Press, 1990), 14.

22. For a more complete description see Gary R. Collins, *Christian Counseling*, rev. ed. (Dallas: Word, 1988), 513.

23. Centers for Disease Control, "Sexual Behavior Among High School Students—United States, 1990," *Morbidity and Mortality Weekly Report* 40 (3 January 1992): 885-88.

24. Josh McDowell and Bob Hostetler, *Right From Wrong*, 268.

25. Sadker and Sadker, 489-90.

26. John Ankerberg and John Weldon, *The Myth of Safe Sex* (Chicago: Moody, 1993), 56.

27. House Select Committee on Children, Youth, and Families, *A Decade of Denial: Teens and AIDS in America* (Washington, D.C.: GPO, 1992).

28. Sadker and Sadker, 502.

29. "Federal Activities Addressing Violence in Schools: Introduction," *Centers for Disease Control Adolescent and School Health Page*, 24 April 2000, http://www.cdc.gov/nccdphp/dash/violence/intro.htm (19 July 2001).

30. Ibid.

31. Centers for Disease Control, "Health Objectives for the Nation Attempted Suicide Among High School Students—United States, 1990," *Morbidity and Mortality Weekly Report* 40 (20 September 1991): 633.

32. Roehlkepartain and Benson, *Youth in Protestant Churches*, 104.

33. "Youth Risk Behavior Surveillance—United States, 1999: Discussion," *Centers for Disease Control MMWR Surveillance Summaries Page*, 9 June 2000/ 49(SS05);1-96, http://www.cdc.gov/mmwr/preview/mmwrhtml/ss4905a1.htm (19 July 2001)

34. Barna Research Group, *Today's Teens: A Generation in Transition*, 9.

35. Strommen, 118.

36. George Barna, *Generation Next*, 59.

Resources and Organizations Which Can Help

Child Abuse and Family

American Humane Association
63 Inverness Dr. East
Englewood, CO 80112-5117
800-227-4645

Center for Parent/Youth Understanding
PO Box 414
Elizabethtown, PA 17022
www.cpyu.org

Kempe Children's Center
1825 Marion St.
Denver, CO 80218
www.kempecenter.org

Substance Use and Addiction

Nat'l Institute on Drug Abuse
Nat'l Institutes of Health
6001 Executive Blvd.,
Room 5213
Bethesda, MD 20892
www.nida.nih.gov

Teen Challenge
PO Box 890
Locust Grove, VA 22508
www.teenchallenge.com

Al-Anon/Alateen Family Group
Headquarters, Inc.
1600 Corporate Landing Pkwy.
Virginia Beach, VA 23454-5617
www.al-anon.org
(for families and friends of alcoholics)

Eating Disorders

American Anorexia Bulimia
Association, Inc.
165 West 46th St., Suite 1108
New York, NY 10036
www.aabainc.org

Teenage Sexuality

True Love Waits
127 Ninth Ave. N. MSN 152
Nashville, TN 37234
800-LUVWAIT

Exodus International
PO Box 77652
Seattle, WA 98177
www.exodusintl.org
(Christian ministry to homosexuals)

Books

Atkinson, Harley. *Ministry With Youth in Crisis.* Birmingham, Ala.: Religious Education Press, 1997.

Barr, Debbie. *Children of Divorce: Helping Kids When Their Parents Are Apart.* Grand Rapids, Mich.: Zondervan, 1992.

Parrot III, Les. *Helping The Struggling Adolescent.* Grand Rapids, Mich.: Zondervan, 1993.

Methods and Techniques for Teaching Youth

9

In every teaching situation, the teacher is faced with the task of choosing the method that most effectively enables the student to learn and interact with the subject matter. A *method* is the tangible, concrete way in which a teacher communicates information or skills to the learners. The techniques and methods selected in the classroom will contribute considerably to the success of the teaching-learning process.

Unfortunately, teachers often put little thought into methodology. Many assume the purpose of instruction is to impart information; consequently, the lecture is held up as the primary, if not the sole, strategy for teaching. However, Christian education of youth is far more extensive and complex. Teaching is not only intended to impart knowledge or information, but it is also designed to enable youth to grow in their faith, to teach them to become critical thinkers, to engage them in ministry and service, to help them apply biblical principles to real-life situations, to increase their power as learners, and to endow them with particular skills. Consequently, a variety of teaching methods must be accessible to complement this multiplicity of purposes and learning contexts.

In considering teaching/learning activities, Ronald Habermas and Klaus Issler invite us to picture a carpenter building cabinets with only a hammer as a tool. Besides its intended function, the carpenter uses the hammer to level the cabinets, to secure the screws, to measure and cut the wood, and to apply the paint.[1] We would consider this absurd, yet classrooms are filled with teachers that practice a similar pattern. These well-meaning teachers are convinced they can teach effectively by using only one method. This chapter will expand our view of methods and identify categories of methods as well as the varieties of methods useful for teaching youth. In addition, it will summarize some helpful guidelines for selecting methods.

Categories of Methods[2]

The variety of teaching methods available to the youth teacher is almost limitless. Kenn Gangel suggests it is helpful to begin to think about methods in terms of categories. He identifies four types or categories of methods: *teacher-to-student* communication, *student-to-teacher* communication, *two-way* communication between teacher and student, and *group activities*.[3]

Teacher-to-Student Methods

These methods are primarily monological in nature. They work best with large groups and are most useful when much content must be covered or when the learners have relatively little knowledge of the subject matter.

The Lecture. The lecture is essentially the dispensing of information to the class. While the lecture is, as mentioned earlier, overused, it is indeed a helpful technique when large amounts of new information must be given. However, the drawbacks of the lecture are that it can limit learner involvement, is often boring, can stifle creative and critical thinking, and may promote student passivity.

Storytelling. This method is generally reserved for instructing children, but it can be used with success in teaching youth. Storytelling is effective because it captures and holds students' attention, appeals to the affective dimension, and allows listeners to put themselves into a given situation. The drawbacks are that some biblical passages (those that are doctrinal in nature) do not lend themselves well to story and many teachers are unskilled in the art of storytelling.

Illustration. Skilled teachers often make effective use of a valuable instructional technique—the illustration. Illustrations can bring a message to life, help learners understand the significance of facts, increase the probability of retention, and make an impression on the listener. Illustrations can be found virtually anywhere: on television, driving to work, observing one's children, in restaurants and malls, on signs and bumper stickers, and in books. Ken Davis suggests asking two questions: 1) Will the illustration interest the class? and 2) Will the illustration enhance and support the message?[4]

Demonstrations. While illustrations are verbal in nature, demonstrations appeal to the learner primarily through the eyes. A wide selection of visual aids is available to the youth teacher: objects, models, maps, pictures, flip charts, and PowerPoint™ slides.

Learner-to-Teacher Methods

Creative Writing. Creative writing includes diaries, Scripture paraphrasing, prayers, short stories, poetry, and plays. Students can be encouraged to do creative writing in response to a sermon, lecture, or discussion, or to illustrate biblical truths being taught in class.

Memorization and Recitation. A method that was prominent in Old Testament education, but often ignored in Sunday School today, is memorization. It is still important that young people be taught to memorize and to recall Scripture and other significant Christian truths. Gangel argues that it is "mind training of the highest order and will develop a proficiency which is applicable in the entire development of one's educational pattern."[5]

Two-Way Communication Methods

These types of methods emphasize the involvement of both the teacher and the student in the learning situation.

Question and Answer. The initial step away from didactic or monological teaching is involving the class in questions and answers. Question-asking can go either direction: from teacher to students or students to teacher. Question and answer techniques give the students opportunity to secure further information and allow the teacher to assess class progress.

Class Discussion. The purpose of class discussion is to get students to think through issues, rather than simply repeating back the correct answers. Utilizing discussion in youth classes is one of the most effective ways of moving students toward active participation. Discussion will enable youth to verbalize what they feel or believe, crystallize their thoughts in relation to the thoughts of their peers, and think through ideas that may have been unclear to them. The problems with the discussion method, however, are that it is time consuming, can be dominated by one or two outspoken youth, and participants sometimes digress from the topic at hand. The method is not very effective in classes of more than 20 to 25 students.

Group Activities

Group activities represent a wide range of learning activities that allow students to work in small groups under the supervision of the teacher or facilitator.

Buzz Groups. Buzz groups are generally used in conjunction with another technique such as lecture or panel discussion. The strategy of breaking into smaller groups (usually three to eight persons) is usually implemented when a large assembly of people have received some information or observed a presentation. For a limited time, these buzz groups discuss a particular problem or address an issue. To make this method most effective, groups can report their findings or conclusions to the larger class. Like other discussion formats, buzz groups enable students to address an issue firsthand.

Socratic Method. The Socratic method of teaching assumes that knowledge lies within the learner, and the task of the teacher is to draw that knowledge out. The learner is motivated by the teacher's questions to reason rather than simply recollect. A key tactic in this strategy is to continually seek clarification of a statement or proposition by challenging it with alternative or conflicting possibilities. While the Socratic method is effective in nurturing reasoning and critical thinking skills, it has some drawbacks. First, it is a painfully slow and complicated process as questions move laboriously from one small point to the next. Second, if the teacher is not careful, he or she can humiliate or discourage a learner with the sharpness of the questioning. Tension can be removed by keeping the dialogues short (10 to 15 minutes at first) and engaging several students in the discussion so as not to put a single individual under pressure.[6]

Case Study. In a case study, a true problem situation is presented to the class for students to analyze and solve. Scenarios must not be simplistic cases with clear-cut answers. Rather, they should address gray areas or complex issues with serious ramifications for all possible solutions.

Panel Discussion. The panel forum involves two or more persons who have differing points of view on an issue or who have expertise or experience which equips them to speak authoritatively on a matter. The key to a successful panel is the moderator, who introduces the subject, keeps the dialogue flowing, and keeps the participants focused on the subject.

Debate. Debate is a teaching procedure whereby two or more people compete in trying to persuade others to accept or reject a particular proposition, belief, or behavior. This method will not appeal to every youth, but for those who are up to the challenge, it can teach research, thinking, and communication skills.

Interview. The interview technique sends students out of the classroom to deliberately secure information from individuals that will be helpful in class. The student or students who take on the interview assignment bring back the information in a form conducive to classroom discussion.

Simulation Activities. Simulation activities or games endeavor to create situations or experiences that imitate or feign reality, therefore providing an opportunity for students to learn experientially. An example of a simulation activity would be helping students to understand the evils of racism by creating a mock environment where certain students receive different treatment based on a specific physical trait, such as eye color. Activities like these are powerful tools for eliciting emotions and personal growth but require a good amount of time, space, and sometimes expensive materials.

Drama and Role-play. Drama is a helpful tool for illustrating a biblical event, portraying the application of a biblical truth, or teaching a scriptural principle. Drama is also effective in engaging the emotions and identifying solutions to the problems of everyday life. If you are one who sees drama as too elaborate or time consuming for the classroom, try using shorter skits or reading through plays in class. Another effective variation of drama is the role-play. While genuine drama requires a script, role-playing participants act out scenarios impromptu or spontaneously.

Field Trips. A field trip takes the students out of the classroom so they can observe what goes on in a particular place or situation, or even have a hands-on experience. For example, the class might visit a Jewish synagogue or attend a Passover seder.

Projects. Projects get students into the act of doing. They may take on a variety of forms such as research and reports, surveys and interviews, building a model of something, visitation, raking leaves for a shut-in, or fund-raising.

Guidelines for Selecting and Using Methods

Methods are teaching activities intended to bring about certain kinds of learning change. The method itself is neither effective nor ineffective. Teaching effectiveness, to a large degree, depends on the teacher's ability to select and use the method that is best able to accomplish his or her purposes. What the best or most appropriate method is for a particular situation depends on a number of variables. Here are some tips for selecting and using methods:

Select methods which best aid you in achieving your aim or objective. It is helpful to prepare the content of the lesson first so you have a clear idea of what you want to accomplish. The clearer and more specific your aims, the easier it is to select your methods.

Choose methods that are suitable for the age group you are teaching. Techniques which require deeper or more reflective thinking are more appropriate for older youth than for students in junior high school.

Be sure to select methods or techniques that you, the teacher, are qualified to use. Make sure you have the skills to make the best use of the method and are comfortable with using the method itself.

Select methods that are approriate to the setting. For example, some techniques will not work well if the group is too large or too small. Lectures are not as effective with 3 or 4 people as they are with a group of 20 or more. Similarly, extremely large groups limit the effectual use of two-way communication or group-centered methods. Also consider such factors as the nature of the content and time available for use of the method.

Be sure to consider the availability of instructional resources needed for the method. It does not help, for example, to have a number of creative overheads to show if an overhead projector is unavailable.

Utilize a variety of methods. It is said that the only poor method of teaching is the one used all the time. A teacher should not only use variety in a particular class session but over the quarter or year.

Arrange the facilities to fit the desired method. For example, small group discussions require the students to sit in small circles. If the room cannot be arranged to fit the method, the teacher is challenged to develop and employ methods that fit the available facilities.

Conclusion

Each time teachers enter the classroom they are presented with new opportunities to challenge youth to learn and develop. The variety of methods available to teachers along with the characteristics of young people combine to form dynamic possibilities in teaching for life change. Youth teachers can choose from various categories of methods and techniques depending on variables such as lesson aims, age and maturity of the learners, the teacher's abilities, setting, and instructional tools and facilities. Under the enabling and guidance of the Holy Spirit, teachers will use methods to create powerful and energetic settings for learning.

For Further Discussion

1. What are the drawbacks of viewing the lecture method (or any other method) as the sole strategy for teaching?
2. Which category of methods are you most comfortable using? Least comfortable? Why?
3. Pick a method that is new or interesting to you and research it further. Plan to try it in a teaching setting.

Notes

1. Ronald Habermas and Klaus Issler, *Teaching for Reconciliation* (Grand Rapids, Mich.: Baker, 1992),146.
2. For more extensive treatments of methodology see Kennneth O. Gangel, *24 Ways to Improve Your Teaching;* Jonathan Thigpen, ed., *Teaching Techniques;* and Marlene D. LeFever, *Creative Teaching Methods.*
3. Gangel, 9-10.
4. Ken Davis, *How to Speak to Youth,* 53.
5. Gangel, 84-85.
6. Ronald T. Hyman, *Ways of Teaching,* 90-118.

Teaching Youth
Through Small Groups

10

The *small group* is a teaching and discipling technique that is so pervasive in youth ministry today that it deserves special attention here. Small groups are everywhere in church ministries—and youth ministry is no exception. In fact, small groups have been lauded as "the most essential tool for discipleship in youth ministry today."[1] There are a variety of types of small groups available to the youth worker, but in keeping with the teaching focus of this book, we will limit our interest to discussion and Bible study groups.

The Value of Small Groups

Why are discussion and Bible study groups such an integral part of youth ministry strategies? How are they beneficial in nurturing youth towards maturity in Christ? Small groups are of great value for a number of reasons.

Small groups provide teenagers an opportunity for relational intimacy.[2] Many youth today feel lonely and alienated and find that meaningful interpersonal relationships are often rare. Because of their size, small groups provide a context where teenagers can be known and loved.

Small groups provide a safe context where teenagers can talk freely. Group members can feel free to ask questions without feeling foolish or fearing criticism.

Small groups encourage the interactive exploration of ideas and opinions.[3] Traditional approaches to education tend to emphasize a passing on of information from teacher to learner. Teenagers, however, are particularly needful of opportunities that allow them to address relevant issues and tough questions in the context of interactive discussions.

Small Bible study groups are one of the most effective tools to help youth teachers fulfill the Great Commission to make disciples. Because of the dynamics of the aforementioned contributions, small group studies are critical in nurturing teenagers towards spiritual maturity.

The Key to Good Discussion: Questions

The primary task of the small group leader is to enable group members to discover biblical truths for themselves. This means the leader must develop the skill of asking good questions.

Good Discussion Questions

What kinds of questions stimulate discussion and enable youth to become discoverers?

Good questions are clear and concise. Questions that are succinctly stated, to the point, and clearly understood by group members work best. Questions that are complex and hard to follow will only bring frustration and silence on behalf of group members.

Good questions are not leading. Leading questions are those which look for a specific answer or are asked in a manner that predetermines the answer. For example, a question like, "God would not look favorably on us if we treated our neighbor like that, would He?" is a leading question.

Good questions are open-ended. One of the keys, if not the main key, to effective group discussion is asking open-ended questions. Open-ended questions generally have more than one correct answer, demand personal reflection, and will nurture dialogue. Examples of open-ended questions are "Why do you think this might be true?" and "In what ways would this attitude affect one's relationship with God?" By contrast, closed-ended questions can be answered with a yes or no, have one-word answers, or have a single correct answer and should be avoided. Examples of closed-ended questions are "Do you agree with that?" and "Should a person lie to protect a loved one?" Often, a closed-ended question can be quickly turned into an open-ended inquiry simply by asking, "Why?"

Good questions are relevant. Effective questions are clearly related to the issue or topic being studied. The teacher must consider the following: Does the question move the class towards the goal or fit in with the flow of discussion? Will the question lead to a clearer understanding of the issue or passage being studied?

Good questions are of interest. The effective facilitator will ask questions that are geared towards the interest and needs level of the small group members. In order to formulate stimulating questions, the leader of small group discussions must understand the issues with which teens are currently wrestling.

Good questions encourage independent and reflective thinking. Group leaders should ask questions that require personal reflection and thoughtful responses.

Types of Discussion Questions

There are three general types of discussion questions, and effective groups and study guides make use of all three in a particular study.

Focus Questions: Group discussions should be launched with one or two questions that serve as ice-breakers and help the group focus on the topic or Scripture passage to be studied. Generally, these questions invite group members to tell a little about themselves. The *Serendipity New Testament* [4] provides excellent focus questions for every passage of the New Testament. Here are several examples: "What do you like best about returning home after a long trip?" or "If you could be king or queen for a day, what new law would you enact?" or "If you could take a cruise anywhere, where would you go?"

Discovery Questions: Discovery questions are of two kinds: *fact* and *interpretation.* Fact questions ask, "What does it say?" and interpretation questions ask, "What does it mean?" Fact-oriented questions often have a single right answer that is clearly evident from the Scripture passage. This, however, goes against the important principle of avoiding questions with a single right answer (or a closed-ended question) and places the burden on the leader to shape questions that still make the participants think. For example, a teacher might ask, "According to John 13:6-9, 36-7, what type of person is Peter?" The correct answer is in the text, but the query requires the youth to do some reflective exploration.

Interpretation questions require some additional wrestling and digging. A teacher may have to do word studies, research the context of the passage, or explore the cultural setting in greater detail. Here are two examples of an interpretation question: "In light of Matthew 16:5-12, what is the 'yeast' about which Jesus warns?" and "What does it mean to 'have been raised with Christ'?" (Col. 3:1).

Response Questions: The third type of question entreats the youth to apply the scriptural lessons to their personal lives. Here are two examples: "Of the numerous characteristics or qualities Paul describes, which has been a success in your life? Which need work?" and "How can you follow Christ's example of servanthood in the way you respond to and help others this week?"

The Key to Good Leading: Listening

Just as important as the ability to ask good questions is the capability to listen effectively. Good listeners tend to be *active listeners* and possess skills such as responding, attending, focused listening, and reading nonverbals.

Responding

Responding is a verbal activity that accomplishes at least two tasks. First, it demonstrates to the speaker that the other person is indeed listening, and second, it helps both the speaker and listener better understand what is being said. Responding occurs through the following actions:

Clarification (e.g., "I am not sure what you mean by that. Could you restate that and tell me a little bit more?");

Paraphrasing (putting into one's own words what the speaker said);

Verbal comments (e.g., "That's interesting," "I'll bet that hurt," "yes," "uh huh");

Summarizing (reviewing and highlighting what has been said).

Attending

Attending is the nonverbal skill of letting the speaker know a listener is with him or her. It is the way one orients oneself both physically and psychologically to the other person. Those who practice careful attending can invite or encourage small group participants to trust them, to open up to them, and to disclose personal information. Attending can be best accomplished by facing the listener, adopting an open posture (leaving arms unfolded), leaning slightly towards the speaker, maintaining good eye contact, and remaining relaxed yet alert.

Focused Listening

Focused listening means listening so one can select the significant points one wants to recall later and allow the nonessential points to go. It also involves comprehending and evaluating all the statements made during a discussion, giving special attention to selected ones so they can be recalled. It means the listener focuses on and tries to remember the major points of the discussion but not all the details of comparisons, stories, examples, or illustrations.

Reading Nonverbal Behavior

Sometimes the nonverbal messages communicated by a sender are more important than the words themselves. Thus, for small group leaders who want to be effective listeners it is imperative to learn how to listen and read nonverbal messages such as body movements, gestures, facial expressions, and voice-related behaviors.

Dealing With Difficult Situations

It can be almost guaranteed that as a small group leader or facilitator you will encounter at least one of the problems or difficult situations described below.

Talkative and Dominant Members

One of the most common problems in small group discussions is the presence of a youth who is prone to answer most of the questions or to dominate the discussion. This individual may interrupt and talk without ceasing on issues that may or may not be relevant to the group goal. The resolution of this type of problem can be handled quite naturally by 1) asking for the contributions of others in a nonthreatening manner with comments such as, "What do the rest of you think?" 2) avoiding eye contact with the individual, which limits the opportunity for him or her to engage in discussion, or 3) gently asking the youth to wrap up his or her thoughts. If none of the above work, it may be necessary to talk to this youth privately, explaining the importance of balanced group participation.

Youth Who Do Not Participate

In contrast to the dominant member is the silent youth, or the one who rarely participates in discussion. First, it is important to realize that a silent person does not really hinder the group. However, if the group is made up primarily of non-participators, it makes for a rather difficult situation and can cause the group to be unproductive. Some adolescents find it extremely difficult to share personal or reflective thoughts of any kind, and they should be given the privilege of simply showing up and listening. The following suggestions, however, might help the facilitator to engage these individuals in discussion: 1) make a general comment like, "We would like to hear from everyone" or "Everyone is welcome to participate," 2) look for nonverbal messages and sparks of interest from the individual and interject with a nonthreatening invitation to speak such as, "Judy, were you going to say something?" 3) find out what interests the quiet individual and incorporate it into the discussion.

Getting Off Track

There is always the danger in small group discussions of getting off track from the original topic, or "rabbit trailing" (as it is commonly called). What can be done to keep a small group discussion from drifting? Here are some tips: 1) politely remind the group that the discussion has wandered too far away from the lesson plan or study topic, 2) offer to pursue the tangential issues after the formal study with those who are interested, or 3) suggest that the digression be the topic of discussion at a future time. It may be appropriate at times to allow the tangent to unfold. As the facilitator, you might choose to follow the digression without saying anything or ask the group if they would like to follow the new train of thought.

"Wrong" Answers

Handling "wrong" answers or completely unrelated and "off the wall" responses is often difficult. On one hand, a leader does not want to allow inaccurate statements to go unchallenged; on the other hand, it is important to allow youth to explore possibilities, wrestle with issues, and even to make mistakes. You certainly do not want to embarrass or cause a young person to lose face by bluntly saying the response is wrong. What then do you do? First, you want to affirm the teenager's attempt to answer the question or engage in the discussion. Second, you might ask the individual to substantiate or back up what has been said. Often, when asked to support an answer, a young person sees the fallacy or err in his or her answer. Third, you could solicit a response from someone else. Comments like, "What do the rest of you think?" or "Does anyone else have some information that would help us better understand the issue?" help take the pressure off the facilitator of having to "correct" the false thinking. Finally, you might rephrase the question or ask a further question that would clarify the thinking or stimulate further thought.

Silence

From time to time you may experience a situation in which, after having asked a question, there is complete silence. No one wants to venture a response, and what may be only a few seconds, seems like forever. Silence may be more prevalent in new groups or in the initial moments of a discussion. How does one respond to silence or poor response? First, do not be afraid of silence; second, give members time to think of a response; and third, make sure the question is clear.

Difficult Questions

From time to time, adolescents will direct difficult questions to the discussion leader. For questions you cannot answer, try the following: 1) throw the question back to the group, 2) do not be afraid to say "I don't know!" and 3) promise that you will do some research to find the answer and encourage students to do likewise.

Making Small Group Discussions Work[5]

In addition to the insights offered above, the following suggestions will contribute to making small group discussions come alive.

Choose a comfortable setting. Try to avoid large, cold rooms such as auditoriums or church basements or settings that provide unnecessary distractions. Homes provide an environment that is most conducive to small group studies.

Set up in a circle or U-shaped fashion. It is critical that the leader and group members can all make eye contact with one another.

Avoid the use of sofas or easy chairs. Teenagers can become too relaxed in soft chairs, and these types of chairs can allow participants to become removed from the circle.

Develop relationships with each of the group members. As a leader, it is important to know each of the group members. Always arrive early in order to get to know any new group members and be sure they are properly introduced to the whole group.

Work towards balanced participation. It is important that every group member has an opportunity to contribute to the discussion.

Discourage domination by individual group members. When one or two youth dominate discussion, other members may get frustrated.

Resist the temptation to answer questions yourself. Rather than squelch any further group discussion, throw questions directed to you, as leader, back to the group.

Learn to guide the group in discussion. This means keeping the discussion moving and drawing out the principle thoughts of participants. Ask questions like, "Would anyone else like to comment on this verse?" or "What do the rest of you think about that statement?"

Do not be afraid of silence. Resist the urge to end the silence that greets some questions. Often, group members simply need time to ponder the discussion question.

Conclusion

Small groups provide a dynamic resource for teaching adolescents and shaping their faith. However, good small group interaction and discussion do not happen automatically; rather, they are the result of careful planning, the use of well thought-out questions, active listening, and the effective facilitating of dialogue and group interaction.

For Further Discussion

1. Does your church or ministry place a high value on small groups? If so, how effective are they? If not, what would you say to convince them of the need for small groups?

2. Prepare a sample lesson on John 13:1-17 using good discussion questions and making use of at least two or three questions from each type (Focus, Discovery, Response).

3. How skilled of a listener are you? Think about your interactions with people over the last few days.

4. Have you ever encountered one of the difficult situations mentioned in the text, whether as a teacher or a student? How well was the situation handled? Can you give any more tips on how to handle these kinds of situations?

5. Why are teachers so often afraid of silence in a discussion group? How can teachers effectively deal with silence?

Notes

1. Jana L. Sundene, "How Can We Make Small Groups Effective in Youth Ministry," in *Reaching a Generation for Christ,* 651-69.
2. Ibid., 653.
3. Ibid.
4. *Serendipity New Testament* (Littleton, Colo.: Serendipity House, 1996).
5. Summarized from Harley Atkinson, *Ministry With Youth in Crisis,* 112-14.

Preparing to Teach

11

Successful teaching of youth demands careful preparation. We have considered the challenges of teaching youth, the objectives of teaching, the role of the teacher, the climate for effective learning, the characteristics and critical issues of adolescence, and the effective methods and techniques for teaching youth. Finally, comes the opportunity to integrate and apply all of this information into a lesson plan geared towards the needs of your specific group.

Preparing Yourself in the Word

Before considering the lesson plan itself, the effective teacher must move through certain preparation steps. It is the teacher's task to transfer or pass on biblical truths to adolescents in the way the original authors intended. Because of the important nature of this task, it is crucial for teachers to make an intentional, thorough study of Scripture a priority. This is accomplished through the process of an inductive Bible study that employs careful exegesis (reading meaning out of the passage) and hermeneutics (the rules of biblical interpretation). A teacher must also consider how the truth of the passage relates to students' lives. This will help a lesson to better meet students' needs. It will also assist a teacher in identifying what changes to expect in students' lives as a result. Knowing how the major theme or events of the passage relate to the interests of youth will help a teacher to select illustrations that will capture students' attention.

The inductive method is an approach to studying Scripture that begins with specific details and moves towards a general principle. Typically, the method demands that the Bible student follow three steps in the process: observation, interpretation, and application.

Larry Richards and Gary Bredfeldt add two more essential steps for the creative bible teacher—generalization and implementation.[1]

Observation: What Does it Say?
    The first step in the study process is to observe the Word and determine what the passage says. The aim of this stage is to find out what the author actually said to the original audience. The question of "What does it say?" can be accomplished by asking a series of questions. Richards and Bredfeldt suggest three series of questions.[2]
Setting Questions
Who is the author or speaker?
Why was the book written? What was the occasion of the book?
What historic events surround the book?
Where was it written? Who were the original recipients?

Context Questions
What literary form is being employed in the passage?
What is the overall message of the book, and how does the passage fit into that message?
What precedes the passage? What follows?

Structural Questions
Are there any repeated words? Repeated phrases?
Does the author make any comparisons? Draw any contrasts?
Does the author raise any questions? Provide any answers?
Does the author point out any cause and effect relationships?
Is there any progression to the passage? In time? Action? Geography?
Does the passage have a climax?
Does the author use figures of speech?
Is there a pivotal statement or word?
What linking words are used? What ideas do they link?
What verbs are used to describe action in the passage?

Interpretation: What Does it Mean?
    Once you have grasped the intent of the author, you will want to identify some interpretive conclusions. At this point, one asks the critical question, "What does the passage mean?" The process of determining the meaning of Scripture is guided by the principles of hermeneutics, the science of the correct interpretation of the Bible. R. C. Sproul identifies a number of basic hermeneutical rules that keep us on track as we search for the meaning of a biblical passage.[3]
➤ First, remember that *Scripture interprets Scripture*. No part of the Word can be interpreted in such a manner that renders it in conflict with another part of Scripture.

➡️ Realize that *the Bible should be interpreted literally.* In other words, while we allow for figures of speech and various literary genres, we always seek to find out what the author intended to communicate in his normal, literal sense.

➡️ One must be careful to *distinguish between literary genres* (e.g. between historical narratives and sermons, realistic graphic descriptions and hyperbole, poetry and prose).

➡️ It is important to pay attention to *metaphors and other figures of speech.* For example, in John 10:9, Jesus says, "I am the gate." He is not describing Himself here as a literal gate with hinges and a latch; rather, His point is that He is the way to the Father.

➡️ Finally, be sure to follow the *grammatical-historical method of interpretation,* which demands the reader pay close attention to the grammatical structure and historical context of the passage.

Generalization: What is the "Big Idea"?

The third step, and the culmination of the process of interpretation, is the discovery of what Wilhoit and Ryken call the "big idea."[4] The big idea is the central focus or main idea of a particular passage. Every text should have a big idea, and this can be discovered simply by asking, "What is the main point or message the author is trying to get across to his audience?" The big idea bridges the gap between the context of the text and contemporary living and sums up the text in a way that makes it universally applicable for all times. Once the teacher has discovered the single unifying principle of the text, he or she can clearly identify lesson aims and plan for teaching.

Application: How Does it Relate?

After interpretation and generalization, the fourth step in the study process is applying the Word. In the application phase, the Bible student must make a meaningful connection between the passage and contemporary adolescent living. This step involves bridging the gap between knowing the Scripture and obeying it. Greg Carlson reminds us that if we want to avoid lack of focus in our teaching, we must articulate intentional points of application before writing the lesson.[5]

Based on 2 Timothy 3:16-17, Richards and Bredfeldt identify four application questions Bible students might ask:[6]

☞ Is there an instruction to be learned and followed?
☞ Is there a rebuke to be listened to and heeded?
☞ Is there a correction to be attended to?
☞ How does this passage train us in righteousness?

Implementation: What Do I Do With It?

The implementation stage of study is closely related to application but is more personal and concrete. It is the point where we take
action on the truths or principles discovered. The Word of God is
not to be merely analyzed, dissected, and reflected upon; it is, after
all, a manual for living. Irving Jenson reminds us that the ultimate
goal in Scripture study "is not to do something to the Bible, but to
let it do something in us."[7] The student of the Word must ask the
question, "What area of my life must I change, based on the teachings of this passage of Scripture?" and then establish a plan for imple-
menting that change.

Developing Lesson Aims

Once you have carefully studied the appropriate passage of Scripture, you can begin to prepare for the classroom experience by developing specific aims. If you hope to achieve positive results in the
classroom, you must be able to articulate precisely what you want to
take place. An aim is a statement of what you, the teacher, want to
accomplish in a particular lesson and is derived from the needs of the
learner and the material that is being studied. The unfortunate consequences of aimless teaching include rambling over too much material, jumping from one topic or issue to another, presenting material
unrelated to students' needs, and offering teaching that produces
minimal results.[8]

Qualities of a Good Aim

What makes a good aim? Findley Edge suggests the following
qualities as components of a good aim:[9]

- ☛ it is brief enough to be remembered;
- ☛ it is clear enough to be written down;
- ☛ it is specific enough to be attainable.

Types of Aims

Lesson aims are usually one of three kinds: knowledge aims, attitude aims, and behavior or conduct aims (more simply put—to
know, feel, or do). Most lessons should incorporate all three types of
aims, for youth need to know what God says, to feel as He does
about the truth, and to be in obedience to what He says.

Knowledge aim. A knowledge aim is concerned with the mastery
of the Bible material. An example of a knowledge aim is as follows:
"The youth will be able to identify ways in which Jesus broke down
barriers in communicating with the woman at the well."

Attitude aim. An attitude aim seeks to lead youth into an appreciation of or a commitment to a Christian ideal or principle. Here is an example of an attitude aim: "The student will develop a greater passion for the unsaved."

Behavior aim. A behavior or conduct response aim calls students to carry out a specific action in daily life. An example of a behavior aim is "The student will write a letter to a parent expressing appreciation for something that parent has done."

Planning the Classroom Experience

The actual classroom learning experience enables you to accomplish the aim or aims you have established. To make the learning experience as meaningful and purposeful as possible, it is imperative that you have a plan of action. Army generals need battle plans, coaches need game plans, and youth teachers need lesson plans, as Richards and Bredfeldt rightly remind us.[10]

Publishers of Christian education curriculum all have particular strategies for planning the classroom experience. One of the most popular models for writing a lesson is the HBLT approach, developed by Larry Richards. HBLT stands for Hook, Book, Look, Took.[11]

Hook: The Lesson Approach

When teenagers walk into the classroom they are usually preoccupied with other things. Their minds and hearts are hardly prepared for a Bible lesson. Thus, it is the responsibility of the teacher to grab their attention from the very start of the classroom experience. The **Hook** is designed to do just that. Just as the fisherman uses a hook to get a fish from the water into the boat, the teacher uses a hook to bring students' minds and hearts into the Bible lesson. A hook might be a provocative question, a video clip, a contemporary song (Christian or secular), an object lesson, a human interest or current event story, or a skit. Whatever the hook is, it must accomplish the following:

☛ it must get the attention of the youth;
☛ it must identify a need;
☛ it must set the direction of the classroom experience;
☛ it should lead naturally into the study of the Word.

Book: The Lesson Development

The Hook grabs the students' attention and gives them a sense of direction as they move into God's Word. In the **Book** section, you will set forth learning experiences that enable your students to investigate, discover, and understand what the Bible says. You and your students will be focusing on the key verse or passage for the lesson.

It is at this point in your preparation that the many types of teaching methods and techniques become valuable (see chapter 9). Choose well by selecting only those techniques that will most readily help you achieve your lesson aims and that will work best with your particular group of students. Be creative, but be sure to plan ahead so that necessary materials, resources, and tools can be secured.

At this point, the learning process for adolescents becomes a critical issue. To merely tell the lesson or to present the truths in lecture format may not be entirely acceptable for youth. Remember that since your students are increasing in their reasoning abilities, they will need activities that stimulate thought and allow them to discover truth for themselves.

Look: The Lesson Application

Lessons must never end at the Bible knowledge and understanding stage. It is critical that lesson application and response be a part of every class session. During the **Look** step, each student is encouraged to ask, "How does the Bible truth apply to *my* life?" Too often in our teaching, we are satisfied with students gaining only a head knowledge of the Word. Instead, we need to give God's Spirit opportunity to impress truth not only on the mind but in the heart and life of each student as well. Without practical, personal application the lesson is mere head knowledge, and the students will be "always learning but never able to acknowledge the truth" (2 Tim. 3:7). "Acknowledging the truth" means allowing God to reveal to the individual where His Word can be personally applied to result in a transformed will and a changed life. A teacher can do this by providing students with an opportunity to consider situations or experiences in which they need to act upon the truth presented.

Took: The Lesson Response

This is the actual response students make to the lesson. After the students have considered the practice of truth, it is the teacher's responsibility to prevent the lesson from dying in the classroom. This is accomplished by engaging students in carry-over activities that allow them to try out the truth, applying it in specific ways to their own lives. It is best the youth identify the specific area of their lives in which they will attempt to use what they have learned. Encourage students to write or in some way identify a specific course of action they will take in using what they have learned. Some examples of a lesson response would be a student committing to read the Bible through in a year after studying the importance of knowing God's Word or a student signing a commitment card saying that he or she will wait until marriage to become sexually active.

Teaching the Bible Dynamically

As you develop your lesson plan and prepare for implementation, pay attention to several teaching principles that have been mentioned or alluded to throughout this book.[12]

Adolescents learn better when they discover truths for themselves. Ask yourself, "Am I lecturing too much?" or "Am I giving students the freedom and time to test out ideas on their own?"

Adolescents learn through experience. Ask yourself, "What can I do to give my students opportunities to experience firsthand what they are learning?"

Adolescents learn through discussion. Ask yourself the question, "Am I giving the youth in my class ample opportunity to ask questions and talk about issues that are pertinent to them?"

Youth are motivated to learn when the answer is not obvious or easy to find. Ask yourself, "Am I spoon-feeding my students, or am I allowing them to wrestle with difficult issues and questions?"

Learning comes easier for youth when the content is relevant. Ask yourself the question, "Do I know the issues facing contemporary youth and, more specifically, the teenagers in my class?"

Learning is not complete until knowledge is put into action. Ask yourself the question, "Am I teaching for life application or am I simply delivering content?"

Conclusion

Careful preparation of the Bible lesson is a demanding task. It begins with a personal study of the Bible lesson (using the steps of observation, interpretation, generalization, application, and implementation) followed by an identification of the specific aims one wants to achieve. Remember that each lesson plan should have four parts: **Hook, Book, Look,** and **Took.** The **Hook** captures the students' attention and prepares their minds and hearts for the lesson topic. The "meat" of the lesson is found in the **Book** section, where the class carefully and thoroughly investigates the Bible passage. The **Look** step forces each student to ask, "How does the Bible passage apply to my life?" Then, the acting out of the application is the **Took** section, where students identify a specific course of action they will take in using what they have learned.

For Further Discussion

1. Select a Scripture passage for a potential youth lesson and follow the five steps of the inductive Bible study method.
2. Can you think of any rules of biblical interpretation to add to the list? What do you see as some of the most common mistakes people make in interpreting the Bible?
3. Using the same Scripture passage from question 1, create a knowledge aim, an attitude aim, and a behavior aim.
4. Why are teachers so prone to focus on the Bible knowledge stage in teaching while neglecting the lesson application and response? What have you noticed in your own teaching? Analyze a few of your past lessons to see how much classroom time was actually spent on application.
5. Evaluate your teaching in light of the six teaching principles for adolescents.

Notes

1. Lawrence O. Richards and Gary J. Bredfeldt, *Creative Bible Teaching,* 64-73.
2. Quoted from Richards and Bredfeldt, 65-66.
3. R. C. Sproul, *Knowing Scripture* (Downers Grove, Ill.: InterVarsity Press, 1977), 46-54.
4. Jim Wilhoit and Leland Ryken, *Effective Bible Teaching* (Grand Rapids, Mich.: Baker, 1988), 92.
5. Gregory C. Carlson, *Understanding Teaching* (Wheaton, Ill.: Evangelical Training Association, 1998), 25.
6. Richards and Bredfeldt, 72.
7. Irving L. Jensen, *Enjoy Your Bible* (Wheaton, Ill.: Harold Shaw, 1992), 119.
8. Findley B. Edge, *Teaching for Results,* 48.
9. Ibid., 49.
10. Richards and Bredfeldt, 151.
11. Ibid., 152-59.
12. See Bill McNabb and Steven Mabry, *Teaching the Bible Creatively* (Grand Rapids, Mich.: Zondervan, 1990), for additional helpful principles for teaching the Bible.

Nurturing a First-Hand Faith in Adolescents

12

Have you had that special teenager in your youth group who was active in every dimension of your ministry, present for all of your meetings and activities, willing to volunteer for ministry opportunities, and eager to be involved in leadership capacities? You had high hopes this individual would go on to be a spiritual dynamo at college or in some way go out and make things happen for the Kingdom. You were disappointed, however, to find that upon graduation from your youth class, this person seemed to fizzle in his or her spiritual walk. What happened? Is it possible that your star student never really cultivated a faith of his or her own?

The overarching purpose of youth ministry is to make disciples, and enveloped in the process of disciple-making is the task of spiritual development or faith formation. For this reason, one of the critical responsibilities of the youth teacher is to enable Christian youth to work towards personalizing their faith, or coming to the point where they possess a faith of their own.

What is Faith?

Faith has already been defined in chapter 6 as the response of the individual to the redemptive work of the Holy Spirit in his or her heart. This response includes all dimensions of one's personhood: intellect, emotion, and volition or will. True faith includes having the right knowledge about God. One must hold firmly to core Christian beliefs. True faith is also having the right passions and motives. One must desire what God desires and have a heartfelt response of love to the One who has redeemed us. Finally, the crowning aspect of faith, as Perry Downs puts it, is the volitional.[1] It is the choice of the will to act out in obedience through one's lifestyle that which is believed and valued. Jesus refers to this dimension of faith when He says, "If you love me, you will obey what I command" (John 14:15). The urgent implication for youth teachers nurturing faith formation in the lives of teenagers is to ensure there is balanced attention given to all three aspects of faith—faith as knowledge (or knowing), faith as conviction (or feeling), and faith as practice (or doing).

Marks of Faith Maturity

Collectively, these three components of faith (knowing, feeling, and doing) give us a holistic view of biblical faith—but are there more specific expressions of faith that demonstrate spiritual maturity? Eugene Roehlkepartain, along with other members of the Search Institute, have identified eight expressions of faith that might give us a well-rounded portrait of a youth with faith maturity.[2] They also serve as guideposts to the teacher who endeavors to teach for faith formation in the lives of his or her students.

Trusting and Believing: Teenagers of mature faith trust in God's saving grace and hold firmly to theological truths such as the divinity and humanity of Christ, God's unconditional love, God's transcendence and immanence, and God's reconciliation to mankind.

Experiencing the Fruits of Faith: Youth who have a mature faith experience a sense of peace, security, and personal well-being that grows out of their faith. It is the fullness of life spoken of in John 10:10.

Integrating Faith and Life: A mature faith is one that shapes all dimensions of life. It is not simply a Sunday morning or youth group experience; rather, it is integrated into work, school, play, and family relationships, as well as moral and ethical decisions.

Seeking Spiritual Growth: Adolescents who are growing in their faith recognize they are on a journey. They nurture their relationship to God through study, reflection, prayer, and discussion, and affirm changes in belief and practice as they mature in their faith.

Nurturing Faith in Community: It is in the community of other believers that youth most successfully grow. In this context, youth nourish one another and support each other in their sometimes difficult spiritual journeys.

Holding Life-affirming Values: Adolescents who are maturing in their faith are learning to pursue a healthy lifestyle, to affirm the sanctity of life, and are committed to life-affirming values such as racial and gender equality.

Advocating Social Change: Mature youth understand that an active faith involves advocating change that brings about greater social justice. There is a concern for the oppressed, the poor, and the less fortunate.

Acting and Serving: Teenagers of mature faith not only advocate justice and social change when appropriate but become actively involved in serving others through acts of love, kindness, and justice.

Teaching For Faith Maturity

According to James Fowler's faith development theory (introduced in chapter 6), adolesents are in the process of moving from a faith that is secondhand and relatively unexamined to a faith that is firsthand and personal. How do youth teachers nurture teenagers in a manner that successfully helps them to establish a firsthand faith? It may be the teacher has to move beyond the typical classroom experience and activity-filled programming to help youth nurture their own personal relationship with God. Teachers must provide alternative opportunities for youth to reflect about their faith on an individual basis as well as in the context of the community. Here are some suggestions for encouraging serious reflection.[3]

Excursions: Take your class to the mountains or to a park, allowing students to get away from the normal interruptions and pressures of everyday life. Perhaps guide them in some form of reflection, thought, or personal meditation.

Retreats: Retreats are familiar strategies for spiritual growth, but too often youth retreats are programmed for activity. Consider the idea of having a retreat with the intent of giving interested youth an opportunity for relaxing, listening, becoming refreshed, being strengthened, and viewing life in the presence of God.[4]

Creative writing: Creative writing assignments are particularly effective ways to get teenagers to reflect on and articulate their personal faith. Writing also enables them to stabilize in their own minds what they believe and to touch the essence of their relationship with God.[5] Kenneth Gangel suggests that the most significant value of creative writing is the exploration into self.[6] Creative writing assignments may include journals, poetry, prayers, paraphrases of the Psalms, and responses to sermons.

Directed meditation: Many teenagers appreciate the opportunity to spend some time alone to think and reflect, but to make this experience most meaningful, they need some guidance or direction. As you send your youth off to meditate, give them something specific to meditate or reflect on such as a Scripture passage.

Small groups: Small groups provide excellent opportunities for youth to explore their personal faith. The key, however, is that they are given opportunity to investigate personal faith issues, not simply talk about what the Bible says. It is important they learn to use the Bible to study not only the people and events in Bible times but themselves as well.

Active learning strategies: Classroom procedures that encourage active learning, such as role-playing and simulation activities, help adolescents identify their feelings related to the faith experience.[7]

The use of questions: Various faith-nurturing activities work best when they are coupled with opportunities to address questions of faith. Make consistent use of questions that force youth to reflect on what they actually believe about their walk with God.

Dealing With Doubt

An anticipated part of adolescent faith development is doubt or a questioning of one's faith. Newly acquired thinking skills, coupled with an adolescent need to develop independence, will likely result in some sort of challenging of the faith system they have developed (or have been handed) to this point. While most parents and teachers are prone to see this process as a spiritual problem, it is more correctly understood as a normal developmental phenomenon. In actuality, doubt may be an indication that Christian growth is taking place.

If doubt is a normal part of adolescent faith formation, it is paramount that the youth teacher have an adequate framework for helping teens who are experiencing doubt. Downs offers the following suggestions for assisting youth who are struggling with difficult questions of their faith.[8]

Remind youth that doubt is not a sin. The Scriptures provide several examples of believers who experienced doubt. The Old Testament prophet Jeremiah struggled with doubt (Jeremiah 20:7-8, 14-18), and John the Baptist expressed doubt as to whether or not Jesus was the Messiah (Matthew 11:1-6). Let the youth in your class know that doubt is not apostasy or a word synonymous with unbelief. Os Guinness declares, "Doubt is not the opposite of faith, nor is it the same as unbelief. Doubt is a state of mind in suspension between faith and unbelief so that it is neither of them wholly and it is each only partly. This distinction is absolutely vital because it uncovers and deals with the first major misconception of doubt—the idea that in doubting a believer is betraying faith and surrendering to unbelief. No misunderstanding causes more anxiety and brings such bondage to sensitive people in doubt."[9]

Provide a safe context where doubts can be expressed. If teenagers get the message that doubting or asking tough questions is wrong, they may very well go somewhere else to satisfy their quest for truth and understanding.

Provide answers for some of their questions. This does not mean teachers quickly answer their questions so that doubt can be eradicated. However, youth will want to be assured that there are indeed answers to tough questions. It is incumbent on the teacher to be familiar with some of the basic issues of apologetics, the rational defense of Christianity.[10] In some situations, however, the teacher might encourage the questioning students to search out answers on their own. In this case, the teacher becomes a resource provider, pointing the students towards helpful sources.

Provide the teenager with authentic Christian experiences. While doubt is an intellectual issue, it is important to note that teenagers are very much experience-oriented. In the words of Perry Downs, "If they can feel the truth of Christianity in their family, church, and youth group, they will have a basis that transcends their intellectual questions."[11] Simply coming to youth group or being involved in a youth class where the presence of God is felt, is a basis of belief for the teenager.

Creating A Climate For Faith Formation

Finally, one question remains: how do we foster a climate that encourages teenagers to personalize their faith? There are many things teachers can do to provide an environment that is conducive to the formation of an authentic faith.

Encourage Independent and Critical Thinking

Teenagers naturally ask tough questions as they seek to grow in their faith. Unfortunately, there is a tendency to stifle this type of questioning and to perceive it as rebellion. Instead of discouraging reflective and critical thinking, we should encourage it. Eugene Roehlkepartain suggests that the thinking climate of a teaching program for youth can be evaluated by asking a series of provocative questions:[12]

☛ To what degree are questions encouraged or discouraged?
☛ How does the church handle diverse questions?
☛ Are youth challenged to examine their faith and lifestyles?
☛ Do teachers of youth model a thinking faith?

Connect Faith and Real-life Experience

Contemporary youth are experience-oriented; they want to know that something works in real life. Thus, it is imperative the youth teacher make a strong connection between faith and human experience. Youth must know that what they learn in the classroom can and must be applied to the everyday decisions of life. They must also know that their faith makes a difference, and it makes a difference now.

Create a Strong Sense of Community

Youth teachers who desire to see young people grow in their faith are well advised to build a strong sense of community. Community building is especially important for faith formation because one's faith is never formed in isolation. Julie Gorman insists, "If we are ever to think and act Christianly we must take into account the heritage that is a part of our uniqueness as children of God. That heritage is community oriented more than individually focused. It is *cooperative* rather than competitive. We have been endowed with 'family'; we function in a system called 'body.'"[13]

Contemporary youth are especially prone to alienation, loneliness, and fragmentation. Community provides a setting where they can gain support when they are wrestling with tough questions.

Emphasize Individual Growth

While faith grows in the context of a community, individuals grow at different rates. Some youth in your class may be relatively mature in their faith development, while others may be struggling or have a more superficial faith. Roehlkepartain suggests the teacher do the following to provide opportunities whereby teenagers at different levels of faith commitment can grow:[14]

Get to know each person in the class on an individual basis. Affirm each teenager's uniqueness.

Affirm the responses from the immature as well as the mature. Encourage all of the students to learn from one another.

Employ learning strategies that allow for a diversity of responses. Open-ended questions and discussion strategies allow and encourage all members to participate and express themselves.

Encourage Intergenerational Contact

Another effective way to help teenagers grow in their faith is to assure they have significant contact with mature Christian adults. There are several ways to promote intergenerational contact.[15]

Develop a mentoring program. Intentionally connect as many youth as possible with mature adults who will get to know them, encourage them, and guide them in their faith journeys.[16]

Offer an intergenerational Sunday School class. Learning will be greatly enhanced as people from all walks of life study the Bible together.

Restructure traditionally age-segmented activities. For example, plan a Vacation Bible School or retreat that includes all ages.

Be sure youth group activities/classes have a high adult-to-youth ratio.

Encourage Ministry and Service Involvement

Duffy Robbins argues that there may be no single activity more effective in enabling teenagers to flesh out their faith than getting them involved in serving others.[17] Service, especially if it is cross-cultural in nature, removes young people from their safe and familiar environments and forces them to reassess their values, theological presuppositions, and priorities. A real-life faith will never be completely acquired without active involvement. Mission trips, service projects, and work camps are some ways to help youth make a connection between the faith dimensions of head, heart, and hands.

Conclusion

The bottom line in your teaching ministry is not how many youth you have in your class or even how dynamic your lessons are. The bottom line is whether or not youth are growing and maturing in their faith journeys and moving towards the attainment of a personalized faith. After all, when all else is stripped away, the central reason for youth ministry remains—to make mature disciples!

For Further Discussion

1. What is the danger of a youth not having a personalized faith? Have you known any students like this?
2. To what degree are you personally exhibiting the marks of faith maturity? When would you say your faith became your own?
3. Why are many youth ministries ineffective in nurturing a firsthand faith in students?
4. What would you tell parents who are concerned that their teenager is having serious doubts about the faith?
5. How much does your teaching ministry encourage independent and critical thinking? Ask yourself Roehlkepartain's four test questions.

Notes

1. Downs, "Faith Shaping: Bringing Youth To Spiritual Maturity," in *The Complete Book of Youth Ministry,* 50.
2. Eugene C. Roehlkepartain, *The Teaching Church,* 36-37.

3. The following suggestions are taken primarily from Duffy Robbins, *The Ministry of Nurture,* 64-69.
4. Iris V. Cully, *Education for Spiritual Growth,* 162.
5. Marlene D. LeFever, *Creative Teaching Methods,* 236.
6. Kenneth O. Gangel, *24 Ways to Improve Your Teaching,* 118.
7. For helpful sources on active learning techniques see Marlene LeFever, *Creative Teaching Methods;* Richard Reichert, *Simulation Games for Religious Education* (Winona, Minn.: Saint Mary's Press, 1975); Wayne Rice, John Roberto, and Mike Yaconelli, *Creative Learning Experiences* (Winona, Minn.: Saint Mary's Press, 1981).
8. Downs, "Faith Shaping," 56-58. See also Harley Atkinson, *Ministry With Youth in Crisis,* 52-53.
9. Os Guinness, *In Two Minds* (Downers Grove, Ill.: InterVarsity, 1976), 27.
10. A helpful resource is Robert J. Morgan, *Beyond Reasonable Doubt* (Wheaton, Ill.: Evangelical Training Association, 1997).
11. Downs, "Faith Shaping," 57.
12. Eugene C. Roehlkepartain, "The Thinking Climate: A Missing Ingredient in Youth Ministry," in *Christian Education Journal* 15, (Fall 1994), 53-63.
13. Julie A. Gorman, *Community That is Christian,* 11.
14. Roehlkepartain, *The Teaching Church,* 144.
15. Ibid., 145-46.
16. Wayne Rice, "Intentional Connections," in *New Directions for Youth Ministry,* 64-82.
17. Robbins, *The Ministry of Nurture,* 166.

Selected Bibliography

Atkinson, Harley. *Ministry With Youth in Crisis*. Birmingham, Ala.: Religious Education Press, 1997.

Bandura, Albert. *Social Learning Theory*. Englewood Cliffs, N.J.: Prentice-Hall, 1977.

Barna, George. *Generation Next*. Ventura, Calif.: Regal, 1995.

Barna Research Group. *Today's Teens: A Generation in Transition*. Glendale, Calif.: Barna Research Group, 1991.

Benson, Peter L., and Eugene C. Roehlkepartain. *Youth in Single-Parent Families*. Minneapolis, Minn.: Search Institute, 1993.

Bibby, Reginald W., and Donald C. Posterski. *Teen Trends*. Toronto, Ont.: Stoddart, 1992.

Biehler, Robert F., and Jack Snowman. *Psychology Applied to Teaching*. 5th ed. Boston: Houghton, 1986.

Bruner, Jerome S. *The Process of Education*. New York: Random House, 1960.

Bryan, C. Doug. *Learning to Teach, Teaching to Learn*. Nashville, Tenn.: Broadman & Holman, 1993.

Campolo, Anthony. "The Youth Culture in Sociological Perspective." In *The Complete Book of Youth Ministry*, edited by Warren S. Benson and Mark H. Senter III, 37-47. Chicago: Moody, 1987.

Coleman, Lucien. *Why the Church Must Teach*. Nashville, Tenn.: Broadman, 1984.

Cully, Iris V. *Education for Spiritual Growth*. San Francisco: Harper & Row, 1984.

Davis, Ken. *How to Speak to Youth*. Loveland, Colo.: Group, 1986.

Dettoni, John M. *Introduction to Youth Ministry*. Grand Rapids, Mich.: Zondervan, 1993.

Dewey, John. *Experience and Education*. New York: Macmillan, 1938.

Downs, Perry G. "Faith Shaping: Bringing Youth to Spiritual Maturity." In *The Complete Book of Youth Ministry*, edited by Warren S. Benson and Mark H. Senter III, 49-60. Chicago: Moody, 1987.

Downs, Perry G. *Teaching For Spiritual Growth*. Grand Rapids, Mich.: Zondervan, 1994.

Draves, William A. *Energizing the Learning Environment*. Manhattan, Kans.: Learning Resources Network, 1995.

Eavey, C. V. *Principles of Teaching for Christian Teachers*. Grand Rapids, Mich.: Zondervan, 1940.

Edge, Findley B. *Teaching for Results*. rev. ed. Nashville, Tenn.: Broadman & Holman, 1995.

Elkind, David. *A Sympathetic Understanding of the Child*. 3d ed. Boston: Allyn and Bacon, 1994.

Erikson, Erik H. *The Life Cycle Completed*. New York: W. W. Norton, 1982.

Fowler, James W. *Stages of Faith*. San Francisco: Harper & Row, 1981.

Gangel, Kenneth O. *24 Ways to Improve Your Teaching*. Wheaton, Ill.: Victor, 1986.

Gordon, Thomas. *Teacher Effectiveness Training*. New York: David McKay, 1974.

Gorman, Julie A. *Community That is Christian*. Wheaton, Ill.: Victor Books, 1993.

Grenz, Stanley J. *Created for Community*. Wheaton, Ill.: Bridgepoint, 1996.

Horne, Herman Harrell. *The Teaching Techniques of Jesus*. Grand Rapids, Mich.: Kregal, 1976/1920 reprint.

Hyman, Ronald T. *Ways of Teaching*. 2d ed. New York: Harper & Row, 1974.

Inhelder, Barbel, and Jean Piaget. *The Growth of Logical Thinking From Childhood to Adolescence*. New York: Basic Books, 1958.

Issler, Klaus, and Ronald Habermas. *How We Learn: A Christian Teacher's Guide to Educational Psychology.* Grand Rapids, Mich.: Baker Books, 1994.

Kohlberg, Lawrence. *The Philosophy of Moral Development*. San Francisco: Harper & Row, 1981.

LeBar, Lois E., and James E. Plueddemann. *Education That is Christian*. Wheaton, Ill.: Victor Books, 1989.

LeFever, Marlene D. *Creative Teaching Methods*. Elgin, Ill.: David C. Cook, 1985.

_____.*Learning Styles*. Colorado Springs, Colo.: David C. Cook, 1995.

Marcia, James E. "Identity in Adolescence." In *Handbook of Adolescent Psychology,* edited by Joseph Adelson, 159-181. New York: Wiley, 1980.

McDowell, Josh, and Bob Hostetler. *Right From Wrong*. Dallas: Word, 1994.

McWhirter, J. Jeffries, et al. *At-Risk Youth: A Comprehensive Response*. Pacific Grove, Calif.: Brooks/Cole, 1993.

Parrott III, Les. *Helping the Struggling Adolescent*. Grand Rapids, Mich.: Zondervan, 1993.

Rice, Wayne. "Intentional Connections." In *New Directions for Youth Ministry,* edited by Amy Simpson, 64-82. Loveland, Colo.: Group, 1998.

Richards, Lawrence O., and Gary J. Bredfeldt. *Creative Bible Teaching*. rev. ed. Chicago: Moody, 1998.

Roelkepartain, Eugene C. *The Teaching Church.* Nashville, Tenn.: Abingdon, 1993.

_____."The Thinking Climate: A Missing Ingredient in Youth Ministry." *Christian Education Journal* 15 (Fall 1994): 53-63.

Roehlkepartain, Eugene C., and Peter L. Benson. *Youth in Protestant Churches.* Minneapolis, Minn.: Search Institute, 1993.

Robbins, Duffy. *The Ministry of Nurture*. Grand Rapids, Mich.: Zondervan, 1990.

Schultz, Thom, and Joani Schultz. *Why Nobody Learns Much of Anything at Church.* Loveland, Colo.: Group, 1993.

Sebald, Hans. *Adolescence*. 3d ed. Englewood Cliffs, N. J.: Prentice-Hall, 1984.

Skinner, B.F. *The Technology of Teaching*. New York: Appleton–Century–Crofts, 1968.

Stevens, Doug. *Called To Care*. Grand Rapids, Mich.: Zondervan, 1985.

Strommen, Merton. *Five Cries of Youth*. 2d rev. ed. San Francisco: HarperSanFrancisco, 1993.

Sundene, Jana L. "How Can We Make Small Groups Effective in Youth Ministry?" In *Reaching a Generation for Christ,* edited by Richard R. Dunn and Mark H. Senter III, 651-69. Chicago: Moody, 1997.

Thigpen, Jonathan N., ed. *Teaching Techniques*. Wheaton, Ill.: Evangelical Training Association, 2001.

Westerhoff, John. *Will Our Children Have Faith*. San Francisco: Harper-Collins, 1976.

Wilhoit, Jim. *Christian Education and the Search for Meaning*. 2d ed. Grand Rapids, Mich.: Baker, 1991.

Wlodkowski, Raymond J. *Enhancing Adult Motivation to Learn*. San Francisco: Jossey-Bass, 1993.

Yount, William R. *Created to Learn*. Nashville, Tenn.: Broadman & Holman, 1996.